Introduction

I n writing this book, it is my desire and prayer that you will find hope, faith, and encouragement to understand that no matter what may have transpired in your life whether it is circumstances or decisions that now in hindsight you recognize were wrong. Or maybe it has been the actions you have taken, the words spoken, or the things you became involved with which resulted in a downward spiral away from God and faith in His Word. What I want you to understand from the very onset is the truth that you can find restoration and a new path in life because "there is always a way back." Perhaps you look back on childhood, and the memories are not good; those things which have been etched into your mind over the years have resulted in negative feelings and thoughts toward the Christian faith. Overbearing legalistic rules that are not particular based upon the Bible can leave many with a view of Christianity that portrays only "thou shall not" rather than the real message that Jesus brought "abundant life." Please don't let any of those things hinder you from making the journey that this book will lead to "there is always a way back."

We live in a world that is full of temptations; the lure of sin is strong and deceitful. Its pleasures only last for a season, and then it pays its wages which is decline toward spiritual things and eventually spiritual death. Many of course blame their situation when this happens upon circumstances, the environment they were brought up in, the people they associated with, and the influence all these things made upon them. Every situation we find ourselves in impacts us all in some way, but blaming everything upon outward influences is really to mask ourselves from the truth of what really happened. Stories could be told of so many, of course, that slipped down the road of sin and to all appearances never really stood a chance in life because of their surroundings, their family life, and the crowd of bad influencers that seemed to drag them into the net. All that is true and is played out every day millions of times across our world. Our prisons are full of people who could tell such a story. However, there are others and again many of them who simply rebelled despite having a good family around them, a comfortable home, and good morals that were taught. To go even further, there are many, and maybe you are one who was brought up in a Christian environment where every encouragement was given to you to follow the faith of Jesus Christ and embrace the life-changing faith of your parents, but you rebelled! Perhaps you wanted to experiment with another way of life despite the pleas and prayers of your family. Maybe you have recognized your experiment left you with scars, regret, shame, guilt, and a feeling of "where do I go from here?"

That is what this book is all about; "there is a way back." I want you to read through this book and take the journey as we unfold one of the great stories Jesus told. I want you to see the picture, and my prayer is that the Lord will help me to paint with words that will capture your thoughts and set your feet upon the road that leads back to home. The world is messy; there are casualties in life, but no matter how entangled you may feel, freedom begins inside our hearts before it can work within our circumstances. Jesus told a story of a man who was beaten up so badly that he was left bleeding and dying, robbed of what little he had, and in desperate need of help. It was of course the man who was helped by a Samaritan who became known as the "Good Samaritan." He bandaged him up, took him to the inn, paid for his stay, and saved his life (Luke 10:30–37).

The chapters that lay ahead have been written with the same motive in mind to bring healing to your wounds to help pick you up and lead you to a safe place. To show you, although the "way back" never looks easy, it's well worth the journey. It starts with a decision and then action. My challenge to you is to make the decision to read through this book, because in it I want to seek to dispel perhaps some myths or wrong thoughts you may have been harboring against the Lord and to show you that the Father who has seen everything and knows everything is waiting for your return. Not simply waiting, but ready to welcome you with a party! The first step is the most important, but once you make it, keep going; your destiny awaits.

The story is about a young man who made some wrong decisions, lived to regret what he had done, but finally turned his steps toward home. Let's make the journey with him because "there is always a way back."

Chapter 1

Walking Away Is Never Immediate

Let me first set the scene and the context of the story Jesus told. It is found in Luke 15, and the reason for the story is simply because Jesus was accused by the Pharisees and scribes (religious teachers and writers of the law of God) of receiving sinners and eating with them. Little did they realize that they were actually describing his mission on earth! Here He was surrounded by tax collectors and sinners. The tax collectors in those days were often despised as they were not the most trustworthy people and often pocketed some of the money they collected. However, they were eager to listen to what Jesus had to say. Jesus will always take time to sit with and speak to those who are eager to listen no matter what they have done. It was because of this criticism that He began to speak in parables or told some simple stories to illustrate the very reason He took time to be with sinners. The story we are concerned with begins in verse 11 to verse 32. It is well known as the story of the "prodigal son."

The family members we are introduced to in the story are basically two sons and their father. Their home was probably what we might call middle class; there was obviously livestock, and more than likely it was a little farm that was tended to by servants or laborers and to all intents and purposes a nice environment. They didn't go hungry; there was always food on the table. There was obviously good parental concern and love that their father showed to them. Through all the daily chores and over the years, he had put some hard-earned money aside for his two sons to eventually inherit. He had planned for their future well. Maybe he didn't have the chance in life that he wanted to give to his sons; he perhaps had come from a poorer home and may have known the struggles that families face when there is not much money to go around. Someone once said, "There are too many days in the month and not enough money." Whatever the family situation was or where their father came from, he was determined to give his two sons a good start in life and had assured them they had an inheritance that he would pass onto them one day.

It was the younger son who approached his father with the request for his inheritance. The question that must be asked is "why?" "Why did he want to leave, and why did he want to get his hands on his inheritance?" It seems to be an immediate decision, but we must read between the lines a little because "leaving is never immediate" or should I say very rarely does this take place; it happens after a process of thought that leads to the decision. Let's try and figure out what the prodigal son was thinking and what was going on in his mind that brought him to this point.

He obviously knew that his father had put money aside for him, and he had an inheritance waiting for him one day. He had probably thought about this for many months. In his mind, there was a picture that kept reoccurring. It was a picture of a life totally different from the one he had known, so different that it looked alluring and exciting; the bright city lights and the busy streets were so different from life on the little farm. People lived differently there; opportunities were greater, and life seemed far more colorful and enjoyable. He had known only life in his father's presence and house; now he is feeling it's time to make the break to experiment. The rules and regulations of his father's house did seem very restrictive, while the city life had so much to offer, and with money in his pocket, he could do what he wanted, and his father would not be around looking over his shoulder; in fact he could experiment with sin, and his family would never know! He would be his own man, no longer called the younger brother. He was ready to make his own decisions! Walking away is never immediate.

The great Apostle Paul had a young man with him in his missionary team called Demas. When Paul wrote a letter to Timothy, I'm sure he wrote with much sadness these words, "Demas has forsaken me having loved this present world" (2 Timothy 4:10). Perhaps the parchment was stained with some of Paul's tears as he wrote. It would have been a bitter disappointment to Paul after all the investment he had put into this young man. Demas had been with him when he planted new churches; he saw incredible miracles and demon-possessed people completely set free. Yet at some point, Demas was considering other things; maybe the missionary life called for too many sacrifices. Somewhere on the journey, the world, and its perceived pleasures, etched themselves upon his mind. He was with Paul, but his mind and heart were somewhere else. Demas didn't suddenly get up and leave; he had thought it through for some time and one day came to his decision, packed his bags, and left. It's sad that we never hear anything else of him; he got lost in a world system and missed his real destiny!

Jacob the twin to Esau (Genesis 27) also left home after deceiving his father Isaac, but this wasn't an immediate decision; it was carefully planned so that he could get his father's blessing which should have gone to his elder brother. This wasn't a quick decision; this was a well-thought-out deception. Of course Jacob had to escape for his life because he knew that there would be consequences to his deception, so he had to run quickly to escape his brother's wrath; his decision was not immediate!

When King David looked across from his housetop one evening and saw Bathsheba bathing, the adultery that ensued took place after lust had been conceived in his mind, and he harbored the thought he could do what he liked because he was the king. What the king wants the king can have! Adultery took place, Bathsheba becomes pregnant, and David tried to cover up his sin. I will refer to this incident in a later chapter, but the point I am making is that what happened to David that day wasn't an immediate decision. Lust was allowed to ferment in his mind, and sin was conceived. His sin of breaking the commandment "you shall not commit adultery" and breaking the moral law of God who had been his refuge and helper in so many ways on his journey to the throne was not immediate. Leaving is never immediate!

The world is full of prodigals.

Sad as it is while Christianity in many parts of the world is the fastest-growing religion, there are millions who have left the church; many profess to still have faith, while others have gone back on everything they once embraced and believed. Sometimes, it's relationships that have broken down, and instead of actually seeking the biblical way of putting matters right with someone who may have offended them, they choose to leave. When fellowship with other Christians ceases, then the slippery slope to the world begins. When hearts are not right with God and church attendance becomes a chore and being committed to some weekly ministry within the church gets pushed aside for other things, it's not too long before leaving is at the top of the agenda. But leaving is never immediate. Prodigals always look for an excuse, something or someone to blame in order to justify their actions.

Young people leave for college, no longer under parental guidance, and it becomes one of the most dangerous times for a fall out from faith. They can be bombarded with secularism atheism and a culture that is so different from the one they have been used to at home. Peer pressure can be immense, morals lax, and the environment filled with temptations that they have been shielded from. Thought patterns are formed, and the temptations are always there day after day. The story of Joseph in the Old Testament is very similar, only he was a servant in Potiphar's house, but it was day after day that Potiphar's wife invited him into her bedroom to commit adultery. Joseph had the spiritual wisdom to say no. He was wrongfully accused by a spiteful lying woman of attempted rape and suffered in prison for several years. Despite all of this because he was prepared to say "no" to temptation, he saved his destiny, and his dream was still on the way to fulfillment (Genesis39:8).

Many are the stories played out day by day of couples who after years of marriage together get divorced or separated. Something happened, something went wrong, and one walked away. Maybe it was a breakdown in communication, perhaps through the busyness of life, job demands, and a growing family that demanded more time, and at the end of the day, they become too tired to talk and communicate. Financial problems may be spiraled out of control, pressures mounted, and resentments were allowed to ferment. Everything else had been allowed to take the place that their spouse once enjoyed. The family, the home, and their lives are left hanging by the threads.

The breakdown in marriage usually falls under one of the following categories, spiritual, financial, physical, and of course as already mentioned general lack of communication.

Why did he leave? Why did she walk away? It was a process, a decline in relationship, problems that maybe were just swept under the carpet and never dealt with. The help they needed they just kept putting off, and one day, one of them walked away. It wasn't immediate; it never is. But there is always a way back! I have met many during the course of my ministry that have had Christian influence and a degree of Bible knowledge in their younger days but succumbed to the pressures of drug addiction or alcoholism; all have a story, a sad story, broken relationships nowhere to go, jobs that have been lost because of their addiction. They live day by day feeling lost, wondering around, while the rest of society seeks to chase the supposed American dream. Their dreams are distant memories clouded by the pull of addiction. They wake every day hoping they can make it through. The haunting question that keeps coming back to them is "Will I ever be different? Will I ever be free?" Let me assure you if that is you, "there is always a way back."

The prodigal son only had one thing on his mind when he left his father's house that was to get away as far as possible. This was his moment, this was what he had planned and been waiting for, and when he plucked up enough courage to ask for his inheritance, that was the first step that took him into the midst of a prodigal world. His walking away was not immediate, but the world was waiting with its net of vices, addictions, and sin. It was after he had tasted these things he was to learn—"there is always a way back."

Chapter 2

Inheritance without the Father's Presence

Once the prodigal son had his inheritance, he gathered his belongings together and journeyed to a far country. The fact that the story Jesus told particularly emphasizes that he went to a "far country" (Luke 15:12-13) seems to infer that he wanted to be as far away as possible from his father. So off he goes a few quick goodbyes, and he is on his way. The problem was he had money in his wallet, his inheritance, but his father's presence was not on his agenda.

This was at the very heart of the problem. It wasn't that he was leaving home, we all do that at some time in our lives, but his problem was that he wanted to live without his father's presence. When Jesus was teaching His disciples to pray, He told them to call God their Father (Luke 11). When anyone is truly born again, the Holy Spirit witnesses with their spirit, and there is an assurance within that causes the believer to acknowledge God as Father (Romans 8).

Prodigals become prodigals because somewhere along the way, they got used to living without the Father's presence. Maybe that describes you; perhaps there were times when you loved to worship the Lord, when you experienced the thrill of His presence. Gathering together with God's people week by week was not something that was a chore, but it was a delight. You may look back to the time you gave your life to the Lord Jesus Christ; you know and remember the change that took place in your heart. Others also noticed your life changed as you shared your story and the thrill of coming to know the truth. At that point in your life, you were learning to walk with the Lord and discover His love and presence. This is at the very heart of knowing God. He longs to fill you and thrill with His presence just as Adam looked forward to walking with God in the very beginnings of creation. Those meetings and conversations with God in the cool of the evening were meetings that Adam enjoyed and treasured, because the created was meeting with the Creator. The love of God had provided everything for his needs. He lived in paradise, and God had created such to bless His children with. As the story unfolds in the book of Genesis, sin was conceived in Adam's heart, and the result of his rebellion and disobedience to the will of God resulted in Adam losing the presence of God (Genesis 3).

It is a sad story that unfolds after Adam's sin; he lived without the Father's presence.

The prodigal had full pockets but an empty heart. He had his inheritance but had walked away from his Father's presence; when that happens, life becomes wasted! Someone well said, "There are no dress rehearsals in life." It is a sobering thought, but it is true. We are all on the stage of life right now. This is it; the curtain opened when we entered the world, and we were on center stage. Life is too valuable to waste, and yet we see it acted out day by day with all kinds of people who are from a variety of backgrounds but somehow have never valued the Father's presence.

Sometimes prodigals walk away because they have become dissatisfied with the church. It may be that they attended a "prodigal church!" That may sound a little absurd at first thought, but allow me to show you what a prodigal church is really like. When the Apostle John wrote the book of the Revelation, he records a message that the Holy Spirit had for the church at Laodicea (Revelation 3:14–22). The first thing that the Lord says to this church is that they were lukewarm. There was no passion, no compassion for the lost and hurting; the church doors were open, and they probably had their weekly activities, but it was mundane; it was uninspiring. They were satisfied with a crowd of people but unmoved with the cries of a hurting world. You could sit in this church and never be challenged to a deeper walk with God or to sacrifice for the kingdom. The preaching just kept people feeling comfortable; people looked around and recognized this church was wealthy as far as money in the bank was concerned. It could have well been looked upon as the place to be. They were not struggling to keep the lights on and pay the bills; the staff were well paid, but there was one great commodity missing, and the sad thing is that the pastors of this church didn't recognize it and neither did the congregation! They had been duped, deceived, and drugged into a spiritual stupor by the devil. Week by week they advertised their meetings, and the people gathered together; they sang, listened to the sermon, and went home unchallenged and unchanged. They had learned to have church without the Father's presence. The Lord's rebuke was that although they thought they were wealthy and needed nothing, they were actually wretched, miserable, poor, blind, and naked. The one who should have been at the center of their preaching and at the center of their worship namely Jesus Christ was standing at the door of the church knocking, longing to come in. He was outside, and they didn't know it. He was outside and services went on as usual; the problem was the usual, having meetings without the Father's presence. They had forgotten they were supposed to encounter God as they came together, but they had become satisfied without the Father's presence. Prodigal churches have turned many away from the Father's presence. If church was as exciting as it is supposed to be, then there would be fewer prodigals. When Paul wrote to the church at Ephesus, he included in his letter a prayer for the church (Ephesians 1:17–22).His prayer was such that their spiritual eyes would be enlightened and that they might know among other things "what the riches of His inheritance in the saints are."

The truth is that when anyone turns to the Lord and is saved, God invests within them the treasure of eternal life. This is not simply life eternal in the sense of living in heaven one day, but the life of the eternal God. Money cannot purchase this, men cannot earn it, and this is life that is invested into the believer that was made possible by the death of Jesus Christ. This life, this inheritance, was purchased with the blood of Jesus (1 John 5:12). What a sin to waste this treasure! What a sin to have been given this and tasted the Father's presence and then walk away and waste the most valuable treasure you can ever be given.

Jesus's message to the Laodicean church was to identify their sin, but to assure them there was a way back, He was knocking at the door waiting to come and change everything to restore the Father's presence. This may sound strange, but it is so easy for anyone to slip back from the place where they once knew and enjoyed the Father's presence. The busyness of life can slowly creep in and take over from Bible reading and personal devotions until the time comes when the flame of personal desire to know more of God has been dampened and only embers remain. Sometimes it's a relationship problem; it would be great if everyone who professes to know Christ did as the Apostle Paul urged, that is, to endeavor to keep the unity of the faith, to esteem others better than themselves, and to walk worthy of the vocation to which they have been called and many other things that Paul taught regarding believers loving, praying, and encouraging each other (Ephesians 4:1–3). Sadly, that doesn't always happen; relationships can be strained, and instead of seeking to restore such a relationship, people shy away from confrontation. Gossip can occur, and instead of talking to the person who may have offended them, they talk about them! When relationships are not healed, bitterness can take root, and whenever that happens, Father's presence cannot be present!

The prodigal walked away. The thing was he wasn't even sad and his mind was filled with other things; he had packed his belongings and was on his way, so full of himself and his own desires; he was on his way to taste the world that he had been shielded from.

When modern prodigals walk away from the church and the presence of God, they don't leave with tears; if they were sad, they wouldn't leave! They walk away with their minds filled with other things that have taken the place of God.

The prodigal was happy but heading for disaster! Eager to leave his Father's presence but little did he realize a day would come when he would long for that again more than anything else in life. But before his steps would find a way back, he had to taste the shame and guilt of sin; of course he didn't realize that as he waved goodbye to his father.

The story of the Apostle Paul's conversion was so different; he thought he knew the Father and was working for Him as he persecuted the church, but once Paul came into a real knowledge of Christ, he encountered the Father's presence and fell in love with the savior of his soul. His heart's cry was "That I might know Him and the power of His resurrection and the fellowship of His sufferings being made conformable to His death" (Philippians 3:10). In Paul's seeking and following after the Lord, the longing to know Him was a desire to know His ways, His will, and His plans and purposes and in all of this to discover the depths of His presence. In any relationship, there has to be a longing to be in each other's presence. When a young man and woman begin dating, they don't just text each other; they go to places together, and they look forward to just being together. It's called love. The fact that God loves to manifest His presence to us is because God loves every one of us. The Creator, our heavenly Father, desired to shower upon His creation, unlimited love, and greater degrees of His presence as He communed with Adam. The story of the Bible is a love story; what took place at Calvary, on that middle cross where the Son of God bled and died for our sins, was the greatest proof the universe could ever witness to the fact that God loves us. The Bible presents us with the story of God seeking a bride, which is a community of people who have found in Him salvation, new life, destiny, and hope. The book of the Revelation presents us with the picture of a "marriage supper." It is called the "marriage supper of the Lamb (Jesus)." The church is seen to be in great celebration with the risen Christ who is called the "bridegroom" (Revelation 19:7). We all must understand that God is not seeking a "girlfriend" but a bride!

God has always sought to manifest His presence, in the forty years that Israel wasted in the wilderness journeys; they still had visible signs of His presence. It was a cloud of glory that resided over the tent of meeting (tabernacle) in the day and a pillar of fire by night. Israel's problem was although they had the visible presence of the

Lord with them, they didn't want to go into the promised land and claim their inheritance.

His presence and inheritance must go together. Moses tasted the presence of the Lord and pleaded with God not to lead them anywhere unless His presence was with them. There is something enticing about His presence; it melts the heart, changes attitudes, and thrills the soul. The Psalmist panted and thirsted for God like the deer panting for water. "As the deer pants for the water brooks, so pants my soul for You, O God" (Psalm 42:1–2). The great challenge to each one of us is, "how much do we really want to know His presence?"

The story is told of a young man and older man who both were about to go swimming in the sea. They waded out into the ocean until the water was about chest high. The older man surprised the younger by pushing the young man's head under the water. He held it under for several seconds and then let go. The young man was struggling and gasping for air and asked why the older man had done this. The older man replied when you desire the presence of God as much as you desired your next breath when underwater, then you will know real desire!

Just recently I was in conversation with a man who stood in line with me at a restaurant; he recognized my British accent and asked how long I had been living in the United States. The next question he asked was what brought me over here, to which I replied jokingly, "American Airlines!" We both laughed, and then I told him I was a pastor of a local church and had come over to the United States for that reason. His immediate reply was, "I am an atheist." I told him I felt sorry for him because he had nothing to look forward to at the end of life; however, he was convinced there was nothing anyway, and no God either. I asked him a simple question which went like this: "If something has been designed, what was necessary for it to be designed?" The answer of course is a designer! I then told him what the Bible teaches "that we are fearfully and wonderfully made" (Psalm 139:14). He walked away apparently still convinced there was no God, how sad; however, I had shared with him eternal truth, and maybe God will use someone else to water that word in the days to come, but everyone has a free will and is responsible for their own decisions.

When we consider the truth that we are fearfully and wonderfully made, it seems to me to be utterly ridiculous to imagine there is no designer. Some may argue that there is no proof that God exists, but I find it hard to understand how anyone can believe it all just happened somehow from a big bang or whatever other ideas man has sought to throw into the equation. It's almost like taking a old wristwatch apart with all its minute little pieces shuffling them all up and taking them up to a high building and throwing them down to the ground and expecting them all to fall into place. Impossible!

The truth is the designer designed us in such a way that our spirit would be the part of us that senses and knows the presence of God. This is what is restored when a person is genuinely born again and saved (Romans 8:15–16). To live without the Father's presence is to live far below what God had intended for His creation.

I heard a true story of something that took place in what is called an encounter meeting in Brazil some years ago. This meeting was scheduled to take place over a weekend in some remote area where men and women who had various needs and addictions would be invited to attend. The schedule was pretty intense, and the congregation mainly consisted of addicts, prostitutes, and alcoholics along with others that had been invited. Bible studies through the day consisted of mainly basic things regarding sin and repentance, etc. To all intents and purposes through the day, these people were bored out of their minds. Some went to the back of the little hall just to get a drink of water and ease the boredom and others walked to the toilet for basically the same reason. The day went on, until part way through the afternoon a little guy walked in who was a pastor and announced his topic that he was to teach was the Holy Spirit. He had not been teaching for too long when he told them he was now going to pray and invite the Holy Spirit into the room. Moments later, these people who had previously been bored and uninterested were weeping; some were lying on the floor obviously affected by what was happening. It was the presence of God that descended into that room. The result was they went home from that weekend "encounter" changed and delivered having had an encounter with the presence of God.

A similar experience happened in New Zealand with a group of minister a number of years ago. This was related to me by a friend who was actually in this meeting. They had not seemingly done anything out of the ordinary prior to this meeting in the sense of fasting or praying for extended times. However, suddenly the presence of God came into that meeting, and many started to weep; others were putting things right with one another asking for forgiveness for various things. One man who was an evangelist ran out of the meeting and went up into the hills and stayed in a little shack there for a whole year because he felt he really didn't know God. Another was on his knees asking God to forgive him for not being a good steward with his money. The truth is that he was already giving ninety percent of his wages to the work of God, yet when the presence of God descended, he wanted to give more!

The two instances that I have just made reference to are perhaps not the ordinary day-to-day happenings, but I simply want to stress that we were designed to experience the presence of God in our spirits, to encounter Him in various ways, and day by day to know the joy and peace of His presence.

The sad truth is that many believers become satisfied with much less; they know in their hearts they have been given an inheritance but exist much of the time without experiencing the Father's presence.

When this happens, decisions are made outside the will of God. Destiny is missed, and leaving while never immediate is on the agenda. The designer designed us in such a way that we would know His presence don't settle for anything less. This is your inheritance; the Father calls you home, because "there is always a way back."

Chapter 3

A Life That Is Empty Is
Open for Deception

In using the term "a life that is empty," I mean a life that is empty of the presence of God. People generally fill their lives with all kinds of things. Some become workaholics; they seem to be always busy doing something. Others fill their lives with hobbies, sport leisure, and pleasure. I'm not suggesting that any of these are wrong or sinful, but when the Lord is not given priority, we become open for deception.

The deception the prodigal was under was that a life given over to sin was better than life at home. He didn't understand the consequences that such a life would bring, but then people seldom do. He was deceived and eager once he had his hands on the money, his inheritance; he wanted to make the journey as far away as possible from the old life.

Deception is such that the person who is deceived doesn't know it. But wherever there is emptiness, there is a desire for the emptiness to be filled. When our lives are empty of the presence of God, they get filled up with other things. No one wants to feel empty. The problem is that many turn to the wrong things to fill the empty void that really should be filled with the presence of God.

A life then that is empty or has walked away from the Father's presence is a prime target for deception. This was what the prodigal became the moment he had made up his mind to leave, but he was too busy making plans, packing his bags, and preparing for the day when he would walk away from his childhood home.

Allow me to show you some of the deceptions that are at work in the world; of course anyone who is deceived (as I have already stated) doesn't know it and refuses to accept it. I'm pretty sure the prodigal's father asked his son where he was heading; maybe he even tried to warn him of the dangers that lurk in the big wide world. Whatever took place, the prodigal was not in the mood to listen or take advice; deceived people never are! We all have a free will, the ability to make our own decisions, but the deceived person interprets the one who maybe is trying to help them as though they are meddling in their affairs. It is usual when someone is deceived that they are filled with pride, and pride tells them they don't need advice from anyone.

These words are recorded concerning Satan, in the book of Revelation (12:9). "The great dragon was cast out, that serpent of old called the Devil and Satan, who deceives the world: he was cast to earth, and his angels were cast out with him."

The Bible not only calls Satan a "deceiver" but the one who deceives the whole world!

A world that is under satanic deception is obviously going to be ruled and dominated by anti-God laws and morals. One only has to observe what has taken place over the last several decades and that which continues to escalate on the downward spiral of morality. Sexual deviation from the revealed will of God, of marriage between a man and a woman, the breakdown of these boundaries, is plain to see when governments legalize anti biblical principles. Of course, the argument is why should we observe or conform to what has been commonly called the institution of marriage. The problem is that once we take out of society the law of God and the moral conduct that teaches, then there are no boundaries. This is exactly what is being pushed by secular governments across the world. Once you take God out of the equation and His revealed laws, then anything goes. And that means the world goes headlong into a godless society. People then live how they please. The attempt to take down the Ten Commandments from public places is just another step in the wrong direction. The teaching in schools of same-sex relationships promotes the deception into the future generation.

The breakdown of marriage is now a commonplace. The media portrays extramarital affairs as the norm. The movies are full of such stories, and the TV soaps seem to compete with each other as to how far they can go with making all of this appear so natural and acceptable. The deception is an all-out assault by the forces of hell to deceive the world and bring it into a further mess.

Governments wrestle with the drug epidemic; millions of dollars are spent on trying to stop the spread of these addictions. Thousands of lives are lost in the United States alone every year due to drug addiction. Borders need to be secured, but the real problem is that the borders in the minds of the people have been broken down. The question may be asked, "Why do people need drugs, and why do people become addicts or alcoholics?" The fact is that often these things become a mask and escape from a heart that is empty. A life that is empty of the presence of God is open for deception!

In the opening introduction to this book I referred to the "Good Samaritan" story, it was the man who was left bleeding and dying that the Samaritan helped. Wounds that are under the surface in the souls of men and women are the things that really need healing, and bandages can't help these wounds. The abused, both mentally and physically, who are reduced to feeling worthless, look for a way to mask their hurts. The problem is, that is all they succeed in doing, masking their hurts.

Drugs and alcohol never fix the problem; they just create an even greater problem. One thing leads to another, and before they know it, they are hooked and addicted and find they are crying for help inside, yet so deceived they think the only help is another drug or another drink.

Joseph, in the Old Testament, was thrown into a pit by his brothers and then sold into slavery. That is what it feels like for the addict that they are no longer in control but slaves to their addiction.

The Bible says of Jesus that "a bruised reed" He (Jesus) will not break and a "smoking flax" He will not put out (Isaiah 42:3 and Matthew 12:20). The word *reed* means the cane or calamus, which grows up in marshy or wet places. It really denotes that which is fragile, weak, and easily waved by the wind or broken down. This is a clear picture of the mission of Jesus and His compassion and willingness to restore. To those whose lives have been bruised and damaged by sin, deception, and circumstances and felt broken, cast aside, worthless, and a failure, Jesus is in the restoration business. He will fan into a flame again the life that has become like a "smoking flax" or like a candle wick that is burning out the reed was also used as a musical instrument, but when broken no melody could be heard. Jesus came to restore the melodies of heaven and the Fathers presence into our lives.

These verses back up his announcement in the synagogue of Nazareth when he said, "The Spirit of the Lord is upon Me, because He has anointed Me to preach the Gospel to the poor; He has sent Me to heal the broken hearted, to proclaim liberty to the captives. And recovering of sight to the blind, to set at liberty those who are oppressed; to proclaim the acceptable year of the Lord" (Luke 4:18–19).

He is always the answer to our deepest problems and our deepest hurts.

The Apostle Paul encouraged the believers in Rome (Romans 12:1–3) not to be conformed to the world or to allow the world to squeeze them into its mold. The problem is that the world is not only a godless society and empty of the presence of God, but there is a huge disconnection which leads to loneliness.

Here is a quote from an Internet article I found interesting. By sharing this, I am not advocating decriminalization of drugs; however, the article does point to a deeper problem of the human heart that is of disconnection and loneliness.

"The likely cure for addiction but this is not what you think," said Johann Hari, author of *Chasing the Scream: The First and Last Days of the War on Drugs*.

> Nearly fifteen years ago, Portugal had one of the worst drug problems in Europe, with 1 percent of the population addicted to heroin. They had

tried a drug war, but the problem just kept getting worse. So they decided to do something radically different. They resolved to decriminalize
all drugs and transfer all the money they used to
spend on arresting and jailing drug addicts and
spend it instead on reconnecting them—to their
own feelings and to the wider society. The most
crucial step is to get them secure housing and
subsidized jobs so they have a purpose in life and
something to get out of bed for. I watched as they
are helped, in warm and welcoming clinics, to
learn how to reconnect with their feelings, after
years of trauma and stunning them into silence
with drugs.

One example I learned about was a group of
addicts who were given a loan to set up a remov-
als firm. Suddenly, they were a group, all bonded
to each other, and to the society, and responsible
for each other's care.

This isn't only relevant to the addicts I love. It is relevant to
all of us, because it forces us to think differently about ourselves.
Human beings are bonding animals. We need to connect and love.
The wisest sentence of the twentieth century was E.M. Forster's "only
connect." But we have created an environment and a culture that
cuts us off from connection or offers only the parody of it offered by
the Internet. The rise of addiction is a symptom of a deeper sickness
in the way we live—constantly directing our gaze toward the next
shiny object we should buy, rather than the human beings all around
us. The writer George Monbiot has called this "the age of loneliness." We have created human societies where it is easier for people to
become cut off from all human connections than ever before.

He also mentions in his article that injecting drug use is down
by 50 percent and addiction has fallen. It is interesting that in an age
where connecting with others is so much easier with social media
and the Internet than it has ever been, texting and e-mails are quick

and easy ways of communicating but are no substitute for human connections and being together.

People can still feel lonely and empty of any real human friendship because as the article points out, "human beings are bonding animals." God is trinity, Father, Son, and Holy Spirit; there is community in the godhead. Church is a community, and community is necessary for many things, one of which is the bonding and relationships of believers. This does not take place when people choose to sit at home and substitute the T.V. preacher for personal attendance at a church and its community of believers.

Addictions are the symptoms of deep problems in the human heart. As stated earlier, the person who feels empty, worthless, and unable to cope often turns to addictions.

The deception is that the addiction will provide an escape. That is a deception the devil has succeeded in luring millions across the world into. It leads to wasted money and a wasted life and human bodies that basically are machines, breaking down under the strain. I have ministered to many who have been in rehabilitation programs, and I know the fallout even after completion of the program is pretty high. I have told these men many times in seeking to encourage them that "their history is not their destiny." On graduating the program, the great need is to become accountable to others, to find fellowship in a good Bible-believing church, and to form connections.

As believers, we are encouraged not to forsake the assembling of ourselves together as we see and understand the last days are upon us. It seems obvious that for such encouragement, the last days prior to the return of Jesus Christ will be marked with even greater deception by the devil himself.

The prodigal son was walking away from good connections and had decided to "go it alone." He was walking away from his father's presence and was open for deception!

The devil has succeeded in sowing deception in the religious world that many now ask, "Which religion is right?" There all kinds of weird beliefs floating around, and sadly, deceived people embrace them. I remember visiting a young man years ago who was the husband of one of the young women who attended our church. He had got involved in some mystic religion that denied the existence of just about everything. He told me the chair I was sitting on was not actually real! It felt pretty real to me it was holding me up, but there was no way I could convince him he was wrong. He was deceived, and the deceived person doesn't know it. We have all kinds of New Age theories that basically teach you can almost believe anything and that there are many ways to eternal life. I am always amazed that some of the most so-called successful people in the world get hooked up with the most bizarre beliefs and are willing to invest millions of dollars into the same. The deception is so real that people give not only their money but their time, energy, and lives to deceptions that have been sowed into the world by the devil himself. It only proves that basically deep down in the human heart people search for a deeper meaning to life but get deceived on the journey. The devil has succeeded in deceiving some people to accept his lie that there is no God and others to believe the deception that there are many ways to reach God.

Let me make it clear at this point that Jesus declared that there is only one way to God the Father and that is through Him, the one who is the way, the truth, and the life (John 14:6). He is the one who died for our sins and actually rose again the third day. No other self-styled prophet ever did this. Christianity stands alone from any other religion; it offers grace and not works. Every other religion demands works to earn eternal life. Christianity also stands upon the truth of the resurrection of Jesus Christ.

Allow me to share with you just one more way that the devil sows deception. I received a call at my office one day; it was a man who asked if we did grief counseling at our church. I told him we did and invited him to come and talk with me so that I may help; his voice was quivering as he spoke to me, and it was pretty obvious that he was in need of some help. He came to my office several days later and related his story. It was his son who had died in his early thirties. Often the grieving person looks back and wonders if only they had done this or said that and they push themselves into a guilt trap. He wept as he relayed the story. It was accidental death due to a mixture of prescription drugs. I spoke with him for a couple of hours that morning and felt I had really helped him with some of the things I had shared. He then asked if he could relay a story that had happened since his son's death that he wanted my opinion on. His son had been, among other things, an artist and had a friend who was also an artist. Several weeks after his son's death had occurred, his son's friend called the father and asked if he could send a photo of his son, and he would do a portrait of him and send it in the mail as soon as he had finished it.

It was several weeks later when the phone rang and the friend told the father that he was going to FedEx the portrait and it would arrive within a few days. It was a summer day, and the father was sitting in his porch when he saw the FedEx delivery van arrive. He walked down the drive toward the van. The driver jumped out and approached the father and in quite a loud voice said, "Mum, Dad, I'm home!" The father was taken back by this as he had never seen this FedEx driver before and why should he say such a thing? The father continued his story telling me that after his son's death, he had been wondering if there was an eternity and a heaven and had been mulling these things around in his mind with no answers seemingly coming to him. The FedEx driver after saying this with a smile on his face turned around and drove away. The father quickly went into the house and asked his wife if she had heard what had been said. She too had heard the driver. The reason I tell you this story is because of what happened next. The father told me that although what he did he now knows was wrong but simply wanted to ask me what I thought. It was a few days later that he contacted a clairvoyant!

Although not at all impressed with the conversation he had with this clairvoyant over the phone, he also knew that the Bible warns against such things and seeking to contact the dead (Deuteronomy 18:10–12). I spoke to him very gently but sought to impress upon him how it is easy to be deceived and caught up in such things, especially when grieving. I pointed him to the Bible and the fact that God is the god of comfort and encouraged him to trust the Lord and that there is eternity and there is a way to be absolutely sure of a home in heaven one day by trusting in the Lord Jesus. We prayed together, and he left my office thanking me for the time spent with him and how he felt it had helped him. As he left, I realized afresh the deceptions that the devil uses. It is the same principle with "spiritualism"; you will never hear the blood mentioned or repentance in any spiritualist service, only the love of God. The familiar spirits they contact can seem convincing, but it is a deception from hell. People swallow the lie because at that time, they feel empty, lost, and heartbroken and are looking for answers.

God never intended you to feel empty but to be filled with all His fullness. But maybe at this point in your life you are experiencing a heart empty of the presence of God. Maybe you remember times when like Adam you enjoyed His presence, but His presence somehow got crowded out with other things.

The world also seeks after wealth and looks for security in possessions, but the Bible teaches that if we seek first the kingdom of God and His righteousness, all these things the world seeks after will be given to us (Matthew 6:33). It is the deception of priorities, and what becomes our priority demands our time and energy. Jesus taught and warned about the power of "mammon" (money) and His teaching on giving and liberality it was with the motive in mind to bring people into the freedom of the deception of "mammon" (Matthew 6:25–34 and Luke 16:1–14).

The word *mammon* is commonly thought to mean money and wealth and is associated with the greedy pursuit of gain. Jesus made it clear that we cannot serve God and mammon. The deception in the world is that it is money and wealth that gives security, significance, identity, and power. But when the heart of man is empty of the presence of God, this deception often becomes the goal and priority.

When the prodigal walked away, his pockets were full; he had his inheritance, but he was leaving his father's presence and walking headlong into the deception that he could break all the rules of morality and clean living, and there would be no consequences. Apart from the obvious consequences that a life of sinful pleasure brings, eventually sin always pays its wages—spiritual death (Romans 6:23).

The other big deception that the world has swallowed hook, line, and sinker is that there is no judgment after death. The world has swallowed the lie to simply "eat, drink, and be merry," and there are no consequences to face in eternity! The Bible teaches the opposite to that, when it says, "It is appointed unto man once to die and after that the judgment" (Hebrews 9:27).

Others are deceived in thinking there is plenty of time anyway; if God exists, then I'll repent later! It's like saying, "I'll take out an insurance policy when I'm older, but many never make it to old age!" The Beatles recorded the song "When I'm Sixty-four," but two of the Beatles John Lennon and George Harrison died before they were sixty four!

The story is told of the devil summoning his demons together for suggestions on how they could deceive the world. One came forward to stand before Satan and suggested that they spin the lie that there is no God. "That will not work," Satan said. "Many believe there is a god." Then another demon came and stood before Satan and suggested that they could deceive the world by telling them there is a god, but there is plenty of time. Immediately, Satan liked that idea and commissioned them to do it.

Deception, deception, deception! The world is full of the lies of the devil and the deceptions he has sown. The deceptions are not all evil in essence but are often a host of other things that take us away from the Father's presence and ultimately leave us with an empty heart. The prodigal had his mind on other things, the kind of things he had been protected from during his years at home, but his departing led to "prodigal living in a prodigal world." It was not until he would see the emptiness of that kind of life that he would entertain the thought that "there is always a way back."

Chapter 4

Prodigal Living in a Prodigal World

J esus described him as wasting his possessions with prodigal living (Luke 15:13). The definition of the word *prodigal* is to be "wastefully or recklessly extravagant." Jesus chose the word carefully to describe Him because this was the life He slipped into. The prodigal was to taste the reality of a "prodigal world." Picturing this story in a modern setting one could imagine the prodigal leaving home impatiently waiting for the bus that was to take him as far away from his father as possible. He boards the bus, pays for his journey, and sits alone at the back of the bus. He wipes the window clean taking his last look at familiar surroundings, but there is no sadness or sorrow; he is too taken with the excitement of another way of life. He would refrain from making conversations with others as he really didn't know what to say if asked the question, "Where and what will you be doing when you arrive at your destination?" The journey is long and tiresome, and with every bump in the road, his memory is jolted with thoughts of his home life. I can imagine him doing his utmost to bury them deep within as he tried to concentrate on what lays ahead at his journey's end. When he reached his destination and stepped off the bus, he was far away from his father's presence and stepped right into living in a prodigal world.

The world as we see it today was never the will or desire of God. When He created it, He created paradise. The devil is described as the god of this world (2 Corinthians 4:4). The very fact that Jesus gave this title to the devil is in itself a description of the world. The prince of darkness and evil has only one great intention, and that is to sow the same into the world, nations, communities, families, and individual lives. The Apostle Paul when writing to the Corinthian church stated that "the devil has blinded the minds of those who believe not lest the light of the glorious gospel of Jesus Christ should shine onto them and they become saved."

The problem with the prodigal was that he had set his mind on prodigal living in a prodigal world. It is interesting to note that in the story of Abraham and his nephew Lot recorded in Genesis 13 Abraham was journeying in obedience to the word of the Lord to a country that he would inherit according to the promise of God. The time came for Lot to separate from Abraham and (verse 10) states that Lot "lifted up his eyes and saw all the plain of Jordan that it was well watered everywhere, before the Lord destroyed Sodom and Gomorrah, like the garden of the Lord, like the land of Egypt as you go toward Zoar." The story continues that Lot dwelt in the cities of the plain and pitched his tent even as far as Sodom, but the men of Sodom were exceedingly sinful against the Lord! (verse 13).

To Lot, everything looked good leading up to the cities of Sodom and Gomorrah; the lush plains looked appealing to him. It wasn't too long after he had pitched his tent toward those cities that he was living in them! He began living in a city where sin was rampant.

The prodigal had pictured in his mind what life would be like once he made the break from his father. For a long time, he had as it were pitched his tent toward a prodigal world. Once he stepped off the bus, he was to start living in it.

What may look exciting is actually filled with casualties and consequences. The world is messy; it is broken, and it exists at this moment of time under the power and influence of Satan. The Apostle Paul wrote to the believers in the city of Ephesus and reminded them of their spiritual state before they came to know the Lord Jesus

Christ. "You He made alive who were dead in trespasses and sins, in which you once walked according to the course of this world, according to the prince of the power of the air, the spirit that now works in the sons of disobedience, among whom we also all once conducted ourselves in the lusts of the flesh, fulfilling the desires of the flesh and of the mind, and were by nature children of wrath just as others" (Ephesians 2:1–3). This is a clear picture and description of what life is like under the influence of a "prodigal world" that is operating under the power of the devil.

Please note, Paul says they were once dead in their sins and trespasses! To everyone around them, they appeared to be living, but what was actually taking place was that they were not really living at all, that is, not in the way that God had designed and planned for them to live. They were being swept along with the tidal wave of a "prodigal world."

Also note that Paul says their conduct (verse 3) was motivated by the lusts of their flesh or selfish motives and their minds that had been warped by sin.

The prodigal was opening himself up to the bombardments of hell.

The Apostle Peter also has another description of what life was like for the believers he wrote to, before they came to know the Lord. He wrote, "For we have spent enough of our past lifetime in doing the will of the Gentiles (non-Jews) when we walked in lewdness, lusts, drunkenness, revelries, parties, and abominable idolatries (1 Peter 4:3). He goes on to make the point that unbelievers find it difficult to understand and find it strange that they did not run with them in the same flood of dissipation, speaking evil of them."

The Message (paraphrased edition of the Bible) renders these verses this way. "You've already put in your time in that God-ignorant way of life, partying night after night, and a drunken and profligate way of life. Now it's time to be done with it for good. Of course your old friends don't understand why you don't join in with the old gang anymore. But you don't have to give an account to them. They're the ones who will be called on the carpet and before God Himself."

As stated earlier, the world is full of casualties that have embraced a life without God and discovered the pleasures of sin that only last for a while and then comes the wages! People are then left with scars, brokenness, pain, and guilt, and sometimes it results in a broken marriage and deep regret. To others it was a crazy night out that led to a fight, an arrest, and a day in court followed by a prison sentence. Too much to drink one night and driving home resulted in an accident; injuries occurred. You live with the guilt. A young girl on a night out in the town has too much to drink, and a young man takes advantage of her. Pregnancy occurs, and she is too ashamed to tell her parents, so she decides on an abortion. Afterward, the guilt comes rushing in like a tidal wave.

The most vivid description of America's present moral situation may be found in Steve Hale's book, Truth Decay, where he compares America to a sinking ship especially the Titanic after it collided into the iceberg. He proclaims, "Our ship is taking on water." He goes on to elaborate more by stating, "We are a nation that finds itself in deep, dark, unexplored waters, groping for answers, searching for direction, and looking for some familiar landmark that will put us back on course.

The problem is that the landmark of the Ten Commandments is no longer a landmark to the vast majority of Americans, and this is unfortunately the same across the world. Society sinks without the moral compass to steer it in the right direction. The world has become 'prodigal' wasteful and recklessly abandoned to sin. The prodigal was about to encounter another lifestyle completely different from the one he had been used to, and another breed of human beings."

But it was easy to make friends. He had money in his pocket; he could pay for a few beers. It wasn't hard either to attract the girls as he shuffled the notes in his wallet. The parties were many. The nights were late, and waking up in the morning with a headache from overindulgence with liquor was a new experience. His body wasn't accustomed to the intake of liquor, but his appetite for it increased quickly. His bed was rarely empty and he often woke in the early hours of the morning wondering who the girl was that lay beside him. He had been so intoxicated with drink he couldn't even remember what her name was!

He was not only partying big time, but he was spending his inheritance on prostitutes (Luke 15:30).

Some women who have been involved in prostitution describe it like it is "paid rape" and voluntary slavery. The woman has been bought, and the man feels he is in complete control of the one he has just paid for her services.

On our travel back from Uganda a few years ago, my wife and I stopped off at Amsterdam for a few days' break after a very busy schedule of ministry. It was our first time in Amsterdam. We loved the quaint buildings and canals and were taking a stroll around the city one evening when without realizing we had entered what is called "the red light district." Obviously, we had heard of this. Amsterdam is noted for it and does not try to hide the fact at all; on the contrary, it advertises the same. Having said that, there was no sign saying, "You are now entering 'the red light district.'" We just strolled along until we happened to glance across the street, and there was a young woman wearing very little posing in her front window. She was looking for customers! Although I had heard of "the red light district," I never thought it would be so blatant. There is a "red light" museum, boat tours that pass through this district, sex shops, and crowds of people from all over the world teeming down its streets. In many parts of the world, young girls get drawn into prostitution because of the lure of making big money. They are often runaways from home and end up in some big city with nowhere to go and get picked up by a "pimp." Sex trafficking is another way that girls get pushed into prostitution as slaves. The world is reckless, and sin knows no limits. It still takes its prisoners and tattoos them all with the scars of shame and guilt.

An article which appeared in the newspaper *The Mail on Sunday* in the UK (February 11, 2018) states:

> Scores of human trafficking trials appeared in the Dutch courts have exposed the horrific truth that many of the smiling window girls have been

brought from Eastern Europe by ruthless pimps, who think nothing of handing out a beating, a knifing or rape. One young woman who had been forced to Amsterdam revealed to The Mail on Sunday; "We are being sold just like something in a shop". Angelica was a bright ambitious teenage student who was transformed into a broken woman aged just 22. As a 17year old she was lured to London by a man she thought of as a boyfriend having been told she would get a well-paid job as a hair stylist. Unknown to her at the other end of the easyjet flight was a willing customer, but he hadn't paid for a haircut- it was Angelica he wanted. Her passport was taken away and she was effectively taken prisoner. Soon she was "sold on" and installed behind a grubby window of an Amsterdam brothel. "The man who brought me to England and then to Holland used me like a piece of meat," she says. "When I saw the brothels with all the girls in the windows, I cried very hard because they looked horrible, and I knew that was what was coming to me." She was told she owed twenty seven thousand pounds to the traffickers because they falsely said her family had been paid off not to report her disappearance. Her three hundred and fifty pounds daily earnings went straight to the brutal pimp who gave her just nine pounds for food. He also raped and beat her.

Eventually, Angelica was rescued when she told one of the support agencies whose staff tours the area that she had been trafficked. But her time in the windows had left a grim legacy. She had contracted a venereal disease and was forced into an abortion, and for a long time, her family refused to speak to her, convinced by the traffickers she had entered prostitution willingly.

The prodigal had never been exposed to this kind of life and temptation before. He didn't know what a brothel was, but it wasn't too long before he did! The girl on the corner smiled at him and spoke in a low seductive voice that caused him to stop and talk. Her invitation to come to her apartment was hard to resist for a young man whose mind was bent on having what he thought was a good time.

In the book of Proverbs 2:10–12, it says, "When wisdom enters your heart and knowledge is pleasant to your soul, discretion will preserve you; understanding will keep you, to deliver you from the way of evil."

Also please note (verses 16–18), "To deliver you from the immoral woman from the seductress who flatters with her words, who forsakes the companion of her youth and forgets the covenant of her God. For her house leads down to death and her paths to the dead."

Proverbs 5:1–9 has similar warnings.

> My son, pay attention to my wisdom; lend your ear to my understanding, that you may preserve discretion and your lips may keep knowledge. For the lips of an immoral woman drip honey, and her mouth is smoother than oil; but in the end she is bitter as wormwood, sharp as a two edged sword her feet go down to death. Her steps lay hold of hell, lest you ponder her path of life. Her ways are unstable you do not know them. Therefore hear me now my children, and do not depart from the words of my mouth. Remove your way far from her, and do not go near the door of her house, lest you give honor to others, and your years to the cruel one.

The prodigal had made his request for his inheritance with the words "give me now my inheritance." "Give me"—at this point in his life, it was all about "me." Selfishness ruled his heart; he had become self-centered, with no thought for his brokenhearted father or for any other people who would be affected by his wasteful, reckless, and excessive lifestyle.

Night after night, he partied and opened himself up to all the temptations a prodigal world could throw at him. Home was becoming a distant memory; it was almost like he had crossed over from another lifetime and stepped into another world. The bus that he had arrived in had become almost like a time machine. The world he was now living in was so far removed from the one he had known. But this world was a world where people only seemed to live for the present and took no thought for the future. Everywhere he looked in the big city it seemed that the motto was "eat, drink, and be merry" and live how you please, do what you please, and forget all those so-called rules of morality. The problem was this "prodigal world" was swallowing his money at an alarming rate! But at this point, he had no thought of returning home. It wasn't relevant to him as he was too involved with reckless and extravagant living and wasn't ready to embrace the truth that "there is always a way back."

Chapter 5

A Wasted Inheritance

The bright lights, late nights, parties, and prostitutes were all becoming addictive but expensive. The problem was in the midst of all that was happening; everyone wasn't smiling. Some were sleeping rough, reduced to begging on the streets; their bed was a cardboard box in an alleyway. Their eyes were heavy and faces filled with depression. The world seemed to pass them by without a thought. The prodigal also could not let these thoughts bury his longtime dreams of "prodigal living." After a few beers, his mind was filled with other things again, and he escaped into a world of pleasure. He had arrived with his inheritance, an inheritance that had been given to him by a loving father, but prodigal living was emptying his pockets and "wasting his inheritance."

He wanted his inheritance from his father, but he didn't treasure it! He hadn't left home with thoughts of investing it, but spending it, or rather wasting it!

The question that must be asked is, "Why do some believers allow their hearts to grow cold toward the Lord, and why do some walk away from the Father's presence just as the prodigal did?" The answer must be they do not appreciate the inheritance that has been given to them the by the Father's grace.

There was no thought in the prodigal's mind of all the sacrifices his father had made over the years, to provide him one day with his inheritance. There were times when his father had gone without, in order to save, so that one day he would present his son with an inheritance that would hopefully provide him with a better start in life than he had been given. His father had made the sacrifice, and the inheritance was a gift!

The great message of the Bible is simply that God the Father sacrificed by sending His Son Jesus Christ, a sacrifice that was born out of love for every one of us. Jesus Christ, the son of God, sacrificed also by coming into this world and dying upon a cross as our Savior, taking our sin and judgment upon Himself. Everyone who believes and truly repents of sin immediately enters into an inheritance that they have not earned, neither do they deserve, but is freely given.

Allow me to share a little of what this actually means. In the well-known verse recorded in John 3:16, we have the word "everlasting life," to quote "For God so loved the world that He gave His only begotten Son that whoever believes in Him should not perish but have 'everlasting life.'"

The Apostle Paul writes of "eternal life" recorded in Romans 6:23, "For the wages of sin is death but the gift of God is eternal life in Jesus Christ our Lord."

The words "eternal life" must not be interpreted to simply mean life that will not end, but there is a fuller meaning, and that is that the life referred to as "eternal" is a different quality of life, the God kind of life. This is what Jesus meant when He declared He had come to give us life and that more abundantly (John 10:10). This is a new dimension of life that resides within the believer and is all part of the new nature and the new creation of those who believe in Jesus Christ (2 Corinthians 5:17).

The problem with many believers is that they don't appreciate what their inheritance is, and it is so often reduced in their minds to having their sins forgiven and one day going to heaven. If that was all that it was, it would be wonderful, but to use an advertising slogan from TV advertisers, "But wait, there is much more." The advertisers normally go on to say if you order right away, "We'll double the offer!" What I have just outlined briefly regarding eternal life is amazing, but there is much more!

Please note Romans 5:10, "For if when we were enemies we were reconciled to God through the death of His Son, much more being reconciled we shall be saved by His life."

This verse speaks of an ongoing salvation or deliverance that takes place in the believer's life as the "life of God" brings a continuing conversion or change from the old life.

Regarding the topic of "wasted inheritance," let me share an article written by Alaina Tweddale for Prudential entitled "Why 7 in 10 People Who Suddenly Inherit Money Lose it All."

There are so many easy ways to overspend, but according to financial psychologists, it's even easier if you're spending an unexpected windfall. Seven in ten people who suddenly receive a large sum of money like an employee bonus, lottery winnings, or an inheritance will lose it all within just a few years.[1] Why? "The way we label money has everything to do with how we spend it," said psychologist and behavioral finance expert Daniel Crosby, PhD. In behavioral finance circles, there's a theory known as mental accounting, which interprets the irrational ways in which people categorize and spend their funds. According to the notion, we're more frugal with funds earmarked as important—like those saved for a child's education, for example—and more extravagant with unexpectedly found money like a substantially sized tax return. "Since an inheritance is typically not gained very effort fully, it is typically spent more loosely," said Crosby. The good news? "A little financial know-how can go a long way toward investing an inheritance and preserving it for the long term."

It is interesting to note that an inheritance that may come our way that we have not worked for is typically spent more loosely! That was the prodigal's experience, and he did spend it loosely with loose living!

I read another story of a woman who had no children, but finding she had ovarian cancer, she wanted to be sure she would have eternal life, so she contacted some mystical religious leader and had her will changed that left all her inheritance to him and to charity! How sad that she thought she could buy eternal life, and even sadder is the fact she didn't know a price had already been paid for her at the cross of Calvary. The Apostle Peter refers to it as "the precious blood of Christ." "You were not redeemed with corruptible things such as silver or gold, from your vain conversation received by tradition of your fathers, but with the precious blood of Christ, as of a lamb without blemish and without spot." (1 Peter 1:18–19).

The Message (paraphrased edition of the Bible) renders it as follows: "Your life is a journey you must travel with a deep consciousness of God. It cost God plenty to get you out of that dead-end life you grew up in. He paid with Christ's blood you know. He died like an unblemished sacrificial lamb."

There is more! The Bible teaches that immediately the repentant sinner turns to Christ the believer then becomes an heir of the Father and a joint heir with Christ (Romans 8:17). The Message calls it "an unbelievable inheritance." I don't fully understand what it means to be a joint heir with Christ in the sense of what that will mean in a future heaven, but it sure sounds exciting. To think that everything God is going to reward Christ with He will also reward the church, to spend eternity discovering the wisdom and love of God and to know that I am not simply in heaven but given the absolute red carpet treatment as one of eternity VIPs. All because of what Christ has done, it truly is an unbelievable inheritance!

There are many other blessings which are all part of the package of salvation the believer inherits, one of which is the authority and access to the throne room of God. Too often we tend to look at the men and women who have moved in great power and blessing down the ages and exercised authority in their ministry and wished we had the same. I often refer to the fact that when I go to the gym I love to see the guys who love to show off their muscles. They undoubtedly wear the sleeveless vests so everyone can see and admire. I try not to let them see me admiring their physique so I don't feed into their ego. But these are the guys who are there every day; it's almost a religion to them or an addiction. I am not saying there is anything wrong with working out, and I must point out that I am not in the least envious! But there is one big difference between the guy with bulging biceps and me; he has exercised and built up his muscles. I have all the potential but haven't exercised as much. It's the same with authority in the spiritual realm; some have used what they have been given, and others haven't used as much, but everyone has been dealt a measure of faith and authority (Romans 12:3). As we learn to use it, we find we have it, and it develops.

I like the story of Queen Esther in the Old Testament, the young Jewish girl who becomes queen. It wasn't protocol for the queen to enter the king's presence without an invitation, but in the book of Esther, she finds herself in the position of taking her life into her own hands on behalf of the Jewish population in Babylon, and the surrounding provinces, in order to thwart the plot of the wicked Haman, who wanted them all killed. She says these wonderful words, "If I perish, I perish" (Esther 4:16). She transgressed a law by going to the king uninvited. This could well have provoked his wrath. Queen Vashti, who preceded Esther, had her royal title removed and was divorced, for not appearing before the king when she was invited. The story goes on to say that Esther found favor in the king's sight, and he held out the golden scepter to her. This was an act that told her she was accepted and allowed to approach the king (Esther 5:2). The fact that Esther touched the end of the scepter shows her willingness to accept the king's authority. By doing this, also she showed her obedience and also acknowledged his kindness toward her. "The righteousness of Christ is the scepter of His kingdom" (Hebrews 1:8). This righteousness is imputed to the believer at the moment of repentance and faith in Christ and provides access into the King of kings presence.

The New Testament encourages all believers to enter boldly into the King of king's presence and to make our requests known.

"The book of Hebrews encourages all believers to approach God's throne, not timidly but with boldness that they may find grace to help in a time of need" (Hebrews 4:16).

The Message renders that verse like this, "So let's walk right up to Him and get what He is so ready to give. Take the mercy and accept the help."

The story is recorded of the famous missionary of the nineteenth century, David Livingstone, who in his passion to bring the gospel to the tribal people of Africa met a tribal chief who told him he could not proceed into his territory without giving a gift. Livingstone had a goat with him from whom he would drink of the milk it provided, because his stomach couldn't take the drinking water. The chief chose to take the goat but in return gave Livingstone his carved stick. The missionary was distraught about losing his goat, but he later learned from a tribesman that the stick in his possession was the chief's royal scepter. With this in his possession, it would allow him entry into every community of the territory. From being distraught, Livingstone became overjoyed.

There is no need of a golden scepter to be extended toward the believer; the blood of Jesus Christ makes it not only possible for us to enter the Father's presence but also allows us to enter clothed in His righteousness. We (as the Message says) have to "come full of belief, confident that we're presentable inside and out."

Also, part of our spiritual inheritance is "authority." We tend to think this only belongs to the giants of faith that we so often read about in books, men and women who did amazing exploits for God. In our minds, we drive out the thought that this also applies to us. Inheritance is of no avail unless we enter into and use it. Without using it, we are prone to wander through life feeling we are the victims of circumstances and "what will be, will be." But the believer has been given spiritual authority which can be used in prayer when we pray in the name of Jesus. This is the name that gets heaven's attention, it is the name above all names. "God has given Him a name that is above all names that at the name of Jesus every knee should bow and every tongue confess that Jesus Christ is Lord to the glory of God the Father" (Philippians 2:9–10).

In the beginning of creation, Adam was given charge over all that God had made. He was placed in a position of delegated authority over all the animal creation; he was to rule the earth under God. Adam lost this authority when he sinned. Instead, he became a prisoner to fear, sin, and guilt and a puppet of the devil. Unfortunately, that is the position of all who have not come to know the Lord Jesus Christ (Ephesians 2:1–3). But spiritual authority has been given back to the church and every believer through the death and resurrection of Christ. I remember a well-known preacher coming to stay with us many years ago; he related the story of a time when he was speaking at a university to a group of Christian students. Just prior to the meeting, a young lady approached him with the request that he would pray and take authority over another meeting which was taking place at the same time in the room above them. A group of students were gathering together to hold a séance. She felt this would obstruct the Christian meeting which was about to commence. The preacher looked at her and said, "No, I am not going to take authority over their meeting by praying against it. You do it. You have as much authority as I have. Use it!"

I have mentioned just a few of the spiritual blessings that make up our inheritance. The point I am stressing is simply this—don't waste what has been given to you. The prodigal went on a binge of reckless and extravagant sinning, and it wasn't too long before his inheritance had disappeared! That is the sad story of so many prodigals of the faith. They remember the times when they enjoyed the blessing of God but over time the memories became hazy and no longer relevant. Life became blurred with so many other things that took priority and left them with the thought that the inheritance they seem to have lost is not recoverable. But let me remind you, "there is always a way back."

Chapter 6

When God Sends a Famine

"But when he had spent all there arose a severe famine in that land, and he began to be in want" (Luke 15:14). After a casual reading of this verse and one would think that it was simply unfortunate circumstances that added one problem upon another for the prodigal. But we must see the divine hand of a loving God behind all of this to recognize what was really happening here. Allow me to take you back to the Old Testament for an illustration of this truth. The book of Esther is the one book in the Bible that never mentions God although God hides Himself behind every word. The book had to pass through the hands of the Persian censor; although it seems His name is eliminated, He is not. The commentator Matthew Henry says, "If the name of God is not here, His finger is." And Dr. Pierson called the book *The Romance of Providence*. The story is set in Babylon, and the Jews were captives in a foreign land, and a young Jewish woman, called Esther, eventually became queen and miraculously saved the Jews from being slaughtered by the wicked Haman.

God who has all foreknowledge sees the future as if it is the present and works behind the scenes in His providence, to bring about His purposes and plans. Divine preservation is always at work and often behind the scenes. It has been well said that God is often doing more behind our backs than in front of our faces. In the book of Esther, as in so many of the stories of the Bible, circumstances happen not by chance but by divine order. In the story of Esther, it was, as previously stated, to save the Jews from slaughter and preserve them for God's ultimate purpose.

In the story of the prodigal, the famine came by divine order to bring the prodigal to a place of want. It is the place of want that leads to the place of "need." You may "want" a drink of water to quench your thirst, but when you "need" a drink of water to keep you alive, you become desperate! Notice what the Bible says (verse 14) "when he had spent all, there arose a severe famine in that land." Now for the first time in his life, he was to experience something he had never experienced before. He had never gone without food before; his father had made sure of that. He always had some spending money in his pocket, and his father had made sure of that too. He had never had the worries of "getting through another day"; he had lived at home under the loving care of a loving father. All that of course over a period of time had become something he had taken for granted and never really given it a second thought. But now this was his main thought. This captivated every moment he was awake; the thought of survival was all that seemed to matter now. "He had spent all." There was nothing left, not a coin in his pocket, his wallet was bare, and he could no longer pay for drinks, hire a prostitute, or join in the incessant party life. Those things now seemed as far away to him as home did! If that wasn't bad enough, a severe famine hit the land. Divine providence was at work. God who loved him so much was moving His hand over the chessboard of the prodigal's life arranging the circumstances so that the only place he could move to was down! That's right down. Before some people can get up, they have to go down. The prodigal had played hard, but now he was to see another side of life, the side where need leads to desperate measures!

To follow this thought through, allow me to mention just some of the instances in the Bible where famine played an important role in bringing about God's required purposes. Most people are familiar with the story of Joseph in the Old Testament, or if not familiar with the whole story, they have heard of Joseph and his coat of many colors. In fact, Andrew Lloyd Webber produced a musical about Joseph's technicolor coat.

The story takes up many chapters in the book of Genesis (37–50), which clearly show to us that God is interested in individuals when only a few chapters detail the creation of the world and mankind. Joseph was not the wisest when he was just seventeen years of age, but his father Jacob loved him and presented him with the coat of many colors. His brothers hated him and were filled with jealousy. They plotted his death but eventually took the opportunity to sell him into slavery. The last they saw of Joseph was when he was being led off by Midianite traders on his way to Egypt. But this young man had God-given dreams that one day his brothers and father would bow down to him. Of course at the tender age of seventeen, Joseph wasn't ready for the fulfillment; he had to be taken through a number of tests first to shape his character. From slavery to prison to the palace is an amazing story. But in the intervening thirteen years, until Joseph reached the age of thirty, there was still the dream to be fulfilled, and his brothers were hundreds of miles away! The great Pharaoh had a dream, and guess who gave him the dream? God who was working in "divine providence!" No one could interpret the dream—none of the wise men of Pharaoh's courts or the magicians. But Pharaoh heard of a young man who was locked up in prison who could interpret dreams, namely, Joseph. Suddenly, everything changed. Joseph interprets the dream and rises, in one day, to become second-in-command to the great Pharaoh. The interpretation was that there would be seven years of plenty and then seven years of famine in the land. Food had to be stock piled and saved for the lean years. The famine was widespread, even to Canaan, and Joseph's brothers and father also felt the effect and severity of it. They heard of the plenty that was in Egypt, and the brothers made the journey because of need! Eventually, these brothers who had no idea that Joseph was still alive didn't recognize him when they stood before him. But they would eventually come to a place of repentance; Joseph would be reconciled to them, and the dream would be fulfilled that they would bow down to him! God used a famine, a severe famine (Genesis 43:1). When God uses extreme circumstances, it is because of His extreme love in bringing about His purposes (Psalm 105:16).

Another famine that comes to mind took place in the days of the Prophet Elijah (1 Kings 17). He prayed that it might not rain, and it did not rain for a period of three and a half years to bring judgment upon the land, for all the evil the wicked King Ahab had allowed. Elijah was to witness not only the miracle of divine preservation during this time but also desperation and hopelessness. During the three and a half years, God had placed His prophet into hiding as the wicked King Ahab was searching for him. Elijah was on the "most wanted" list in the country. He was fed miraculously by ravens bringing him meat each day and a brook that provided him with water that is until the brook dried up! Elijah, at the word of the Lord, went to Zarephath with the promise that a widow would sustain him. He met the widow, but she was void of any hope of survival and about to bake her last cakes for her and her son and then die. The prophet delivered the word of the Lord to her with the promise that if she would first give him a cake, the barrel of oil would not fail neither would the flour until God would send rain once again upon the earth. She obeyed and witnessed a miracle! But what Elijah saw as he looked at this woman when they first met was desperation and hopelessness. Famine can have that effect!

The great promise God gave to Solomon was in 2 Chronicles 7:14, "If My people who are called by My name will humble themselves, and pray and seek My face and turn from their wicked ways, then will I hear from heaven and will forgive their sin and heal their land." Please note the previous verse (verse 13), "When I shut up heaven and there is no rain or command the locusts to devour the land, or send pestilence among My people . . ." Famine came often as a form of judgment in order to bring the people back to the Lord. The prodigal had lived recklessly and extravagantly as far as sin was concerned; his earthly father knew nothing of what was happening, but his heavenly Father had seen it all. Now the prodigal is without money and in the middle of a famine! God uses the natural often to bring us to awareness of the spiritual. For the prodigal, it was empty pockets and no food. God was showing him the state of his heart that it was empty; it had been drained of any spiritual awareness that his father had sought to teach him over the years. It is sometimes difficult for the casual observer to understand that a god of love could allow such things. When Isaiah the prophet spoke of Christ's suffering (Isaiah 53), he described Jesus as a lamb that was led to the slaughter. One could ask the same question, "How could God allow His Son to be 'slaughtered?'" The answer is found in John 3:16, "For God so loved the world that he gave His only begotten Son that whoever believes on Him should not perish but have eternal life." The truth is God loves every one of us, including the deepest dyed sinners and the prodigals who have lost their way. He loves them so much that He will send famines if necessary to bring them back to Him and to home.

Of course, there are two options when we feel we are in need. One is to turn bitter and blame God—which is really masking the whole problem, a problem that lies in the human heart. The other is to turn to the Lord. At this point in the story, the prodigal is not quite there yet. He is still trying to figure out what he can do to help himself, so he went into survival mode. He was not ready to contemplate the truth that "there is always a way back."

Chapter 7

Eating with Pigs

It's one thing to have no money and be in the midst of a famine, but now the prodigal has to go one step further down to rock bottom—feeding pigs! He was so desperate that he applied for a job on a pig farm; there was it seemed nowhere else to go. He had lost his apartment because he couldn't afford the rent. The landlord had no mercy upon him, and before he knew it, he was out on the streets. These were the same streets he had walked along many times on his way to the nightclubs, gambling dens and brothels of the big city. He never had time for the dropouts that lay in shop doorways with their begging bowls. He had stepped many times over their cardboard boxes and piles of filthy clothes which made up all their earthly belongings. He never spared them a thought, at least not a compassionate one! Now he was one of them. He was someone who had nowhere to go, nowhere to call home, and nowhere to lay his head down at night. He looked at these people through totally different eyes. He wondered what their story was and how they came to be in the state they were. Had they made similar mistakes? Had they walked away from security? Had they spent their money recklessly?

The prodigal heard of a job going on the pig farm, and because there was nothing else, he introduced himself to the farmer who gave him the job of feeding his pigs. This wasn't ideal by any stretch of the imagination, but it was all there was. He walked into the smelly muddy pigsty with a bucket of pig food. The first step inside the sty there was a squelch as he stepped into a mixture of mud and pig dung. He looked at the pigs eager to eat and was somewhat envious that at least they were getting fed.

Speaking of jobs that no one wants to do, I am reminded of a true story I heard from a Chinese pastor some years ago. He was ministering in our church one Sunday morning and began by relating his experience as a prisoner of the communists. When the communists took over, many of the pastors of the churches were taken away to prison labor camps. They were under constant guard, and at no time where they were on their own, there was always a guard within a few yards armed with a rifle. A time to be alone and to pray was nonexistent, but when they realized that he was from a middle-class home, they gave him the worst job in the prison camp— cleaning out the sewage pit each day! He would have to step into the tank bringing a bucket, and then the sewage would be used as manure in the fields. He went on to tell us that as soon as he lifted the lid on the sewage tank, there would be no guard within one hundred yards of him. The stench was so terrible. As he went through this chore every day, he told us this was the time he could sing and pray aloud, and when he related what his favorite song was that he sang each day while cleaning the sewage tank, there was hardly a dry eye in the church that morning. It was the following:

> I come to the garden alone while the dew is still
> on the roses and the voice I hear falling on my ear
> the Son of God discloses.

> Chorus:
> And He walks with me and He talks with
> me and He tells me I am His own and the joy we
> share as we tarry there no other has ever known.

For our pastor friend from China, he had no choice to be there; he was a prisoner. The prodigal felt that he too had no choice and that he also was a prisoner who was now seeing the effects of his reckless and extravagant lifestyle of sin and also a prisoner to the workings of divine providence in the midst of a famine! He was in need of help, but no one helped him. All alone and feeling the effect of hunger pangs, he would have filled his belly with the pods the pigs left behind. It is interesting to note that it was pigs the prodigal was feeding. Pigs were listed as one of the "unclean animals" that the Jews should never eat according to Leviticus 11:1–23 and Deuteronomy 14:3–21. The pig will eat anything including its own urine and feces, rotting vegetables, maggots, and even decaying and rotting flesh of other animals. I am not suggesting that you no longer eat bacon. That is entirely up to the individual as Paul says, "For every creature of God is good and nothing is to be refused if it is received with thanksgiving, for it is sanctified by the word of God and prayer" (1 Timothy 4:3–5). However, for the prodigal, he was feeding unclean animals according to the Levitical law. Perhaps God was allowing all of this to show him the unclean state of his own heart!

In the account of the deliverance of the man who was possessed by demons recorded in Mark 5, it was pigs that Jesus sent the legion of demons into as He cast them out of the possessed man.

We have before us a picture of a young man who had now hit rock bottom. He was with the unclean animals isolated from home and with no one to help. He must have felt like the leper, who by reason of his contagious disease had to leave home and family and join a leper colony. He would have to bandage the wounds that the disease had inflicted upon his body and toll a bell whenever he came near to other people; he would also have to shout the terrible words "unclean, unclean." The prodigal's heart was shouting out to him those very same words. His mind was confused; all he could see was filth, and God was impressing upon him that this was his spiritual state! No food, no shelter, and no home to go to at the end of the day and no one to talk to, nothing on the table! It was never like this at home, he must have thought. "My father would never have allowed me to be in such a mess," these and many other thoughts of home came flooding to his mind.

Our heavenly Father is the god who came to shower upon us His love and blessings and to provide in so many wonderful ways. Even the children of Israel were fed miraculously during their wilderness journeys, even though they asked in their unbelief, "Can God spread a table in the wilderness?"(Psalm 78:19). He certainly did, and He did it for forty years until they reached the land of Canaan, a land that the Bible describes as flowing with milk and honey.

The psalmist David wrote that God prepared a table before him in the presence of his enemies (Psalm 23:5). In the "Song of Solomon" (2:4), we find these words, "He brought me into His banqueting house and His banner over me is love." The truth is that God is love, and He only wants the very best for His children, but when like the prodigal one of His children chooses to walk away, He will chase them longing for them to come to the realization "that there is always a way back." For the prodigal, events had changed dramatically; there was a complete reverse of fortune. As you read this book, I don't know your story or your circumstances. I don't know whether at this moment in time you see yourself as a prodigal. Maybe you have gone down a similar road, or perhaps for some reason you have lost your way in faith. Perhaps you too have experienced a turnaround and reverse of fortune. It may have been a sudden job loss, a marriage breakup, or a moment when temptation lured you back to the addiction. It may have been someone you trusted that let you down and spoke words that cut you and hurt you. Whatever the situation, remember God loves you, and He waits and watches for your next move.

If things have happened to you that have been self-inflicted as was the case with the prodigal, God in His extreme love still allows famines or circumstances that are designed to reveal to us the state of our heart and bring us back to our loving Father. But then again, you may not be a prodigal; you may be someone who is praying for a prodigal. You may be the parent who longs for that son or daughter to return to faith. Whatever the category you fall into, please remember "there is always a way back."

Chapter 8

Left Alone

Help wasn't coming from anyone, only a meager pittance of a wage from working with the pigs (Luke 15:16). He had thrown his money around in the bars, paid for drinks, and had been lavish with his payments to the prostitutes, but times had changed. In fact, everything had changed. Not only did he have no money, but there were no handouts coming from anyone. For the first time since leaving his father and home, he felt alone, and the reality of the long distance between them seemed to dominate his thoughts. There was no one to speak to, no one that would understand, and no one who would lend a listening ear.

Many people hide their loneliness with busyness and activities trying to surround themselves with an abundance of things to do and if possible stay at all times in the company of others. The problem is that people can be surrounded with other people, and they can live in communities that are teeming with people and activity, and yet that is not the cure for loneliness. As part of "grief counseling," my wife, Val, and I show a DVD series *Dr. Brown*, which tells the story of when his wife died in her early thirties and left him with two small boys. Each night he would go to bed but always had to have the TV on when he was winding down for the night. One night he decided to switch the TV off and lay there in the dark feeling the loss and loneliness of his wife. He suddenly said to himself in that dark empty bedroom, "Well this is me now!" He had to come to terms with the loneliness, and there are not many people that like to do that. The scariest thing for some is simply to be left alone. The reason is that deep down they are not at ease; there are too many anxieties pushed way down, and when left alone, they all seem to come up to the surface and cause sleepless nights and anxious days.

God who had moved behind the scenes and sent a famine was now bringing the prodigal into a new experience, an experience that would cause him to do some deep reflecting, heart searching that would eventually cause him for the first time to see him as he really was.

In the story of Jacob and Esau (Genesis 32:34), we find the words "then Jacob was left alone, and a man wrestled with him until the breaking of the day." Jacob, as mentioned earlier in the book, had lied and deceived his brother, and in the intervening years since Jacob had run away in fear of his life, he also had been deceived by his uncle Laban. The time had come when Jacob has to face his brother again. Obviously, this was not something he was looking forward to but actually feared. However, it is interesting to find this verse (24) which tells us Jacob was left alone. He, like the prodigal, had never been alone since his escape from home, but again, God was at work. This was to be a night that Jacob would never forget because this was a night when he met with God.

Before his name could be changed to "Israel" which means "ruled by God," there was a wrestling match, and God was the initiator! It is never a good idea to argue with God because He is the Lord and He doesn't change, and apart from that, He is all knowing, all seeing, and perfect. Perfection doesn't change! He is also all powerful, so if we choose to enter into a fight or wrestling match, we are certain to come out the loser. For Jacob the socket of his thigh came out of joint as God touched it, yet Jacob would not let go, and we have these amazing words recorded, "I will not let you go unless you bless me!" (verse 26). Although Jacob was left with a limp, he had a new name, and a new day dawned (verses 28–31); he actually came out better than he was before!

When God asked Jacob what his name was, it wasn't that He didn't know; it was simply to get Jacob to confess it, to say it, which means "to be behind" but also "to supplant, circumvent, assail, and overreach" or from the word *heel*. In other words, God wanted to face Jacob up with who he really was.

The prodigal was now in the same kind of situation; he had to come to terms with what he had done and the kind of lifestyle he had lived since leaving home. It is never easy to do this, it is humbling, it feels awkward, and it's like one has looked in the mirror every day of one's life, and the image that has stared back has been heavy with makeup, hiding the blemishes, the wrinkles, and the pain that has been going on inside. But now the mirror hides nothing. In fact, it reveals everything; it looks beyond outward appearance and reveals the heart, and its motives, the hidden sins that no one knew about. Suddenly, the image has changed. It's almost like the old movie *Dr. Jekyll and Mr. Hyde* (1931).

In the movie, Dr. Jekyll faces horrible consequences when he lets his dark side run wild with a potion that transforms him into the animalistic Mr. Hyde.

Loneliness is often the time when we see ourselves, as we really are; here are some quotes on "loneliness":

"When I'm alone, I think and think and think."

"I use sarcasm and jokes to cover up the fact that I am lonely and have bad anxiety about almost everything."

"Lonely is not being alone, it's the feeling that no one cares."

"You never realize how lonely you are until it's the end of the day and you have a bunch of things to talk about and no one to talk to."

"I feel I'm not anyone's first choice, neither their favorite. Even if people tell me I'm important to them, or I mean a lot to them, I know there's always someone they prefer to be with, someone they choose to be with over me and that hurts a lot."

There is the loneliness of bereavement and the loneliness of divorce. And the reality of a world still goes about its daily routines and seems oblivious to the lonely. The lonely person looks through spectacles that are tinted with grey. That's how the world appears; everybody else seems to have a friend, a spouse, or someone that they can confide in. Days can be long and evenings even longer, and the only companion is loneliness. No one sees the tears or hears the heart cry for companionship. The dark days of winter only add to the despair; all the new technology doesn't substitute for flesh and blood companionship. Loneliness can steal your hope; it can color your moods and fill a person with the despairing thought that nobody really cares.

In the book *Building a Church of Small Groups*, Bill Donahue and Russ Robinson have some interesting thoughts on the subject of loneliness. They write of the god of community, "Then God said, 'Let us make man in our image, in our likeness'" (Genesis 1:26). They make the point of the plurality of God and that when God created man, He created him with the "community gene." They also bring out the truth that the relational "community gene" helps explain why churches need small groups. People basically need connections; they were never created to be "lone rangers" isolated from relationships.

I heard recently the testimony of a young woman who had been arrested for the second time on drug charges. Although she tried to put on a brave face when handcuffed, it was when she was locked in a cell all alone that loneliness hit her and the reality of what she had done. The one thing prisoners hate is solitary confinement; it is used as a punishment. A further illustration is found in the book of Senator John McCain a former POW in Vietnam. He describes the elation he experienced when he was reunited with fellow prisoners after a horribly long and brutal separation:

"I was overwhelmed by the compulsion to talk nonstop, face-to-face with my obliging new cellmate. I ran my mouth ceaselessly for four days . . ."

Loneliness leaves a person with no one but themselves, their thoughts and a heart that crave for relationship and connection. This was exactly how the prodigal felt; no one cared enough to give him anything; he met loneliness it seems just as quickly as he met his new lifestyle when he stepped into the bright city lights. That was the day when he felt he was at last free from his father's paternal care and he could live as he pleased. Now he only had loneliness as his companion.

He had to look into the mirror and see the dark side of his life and to figure out when and what was the potion he took, like Dr. Jekyll that changed him, a potion that had changed him and sought to destroy him and had led to him feeding pigs in the field. He had become so hungry and so desperate that he would have eaten the pods the pigs left behind. Desperate people take desperate measures, but what could he do, and where could he go?

This experience called for deep thinking, something he hadn't given too much time to since leaving home. He had been too consumed with what he wanted to do. Now he had to figure out what he had to do. And what he had to do had not been on the agenda of what he wanted to do!

The prodigal could have done what many do when they are in a situation that calls for a life change and ownership of their sin; they push the blame onto someone else! But going down that road would not have helped him at all. But consider for a moment what he might have thought and who he possibly could have blamed. He could have blamed his upbringing, although that would have been foolish. But he could have allowed his mind to take him on a journey that told him that his upbringing was too strict and too many rules; it didn't prepare him for the real world. He could have thought of his father as being too overbearing and too protective. Perhaps he felt that his brother, being the eldest, always got the most attention and the better treatment and that he always felt second best to his brother. He could have dreamed up a thousand scenarios as to why he was in the situation he was in and who was to blame. He could have told himself that everyone else apart from himself was to blame for the mess he was now in. I'm sure none of those things were true at least; they never appear in the story Jesus told. Even if they were, blaming others would not have provided him with answers or put him on the right path to restoration. Human nature always wants to point the finger at someone else! To go back to the beginning of the creation account in the book of Genesis, we find fallen human nature at work with both Adam and Eve trying to push the blame away from them. Genesis 3 commences with the words "Now the serpent was more cunning than any beast of the field which the Lord God had made.

And he said to the woman, 'Has God indeed said, "You shall not eat of every tree of the garden?"'"

Eve was deceived by the serpent and ate of the forbidden fruit and in so doing lost the presence of God in her life along with her innocence. In its place she experienced guilt. She turned to her husband Adam and gave him the fruit, and he ate too. It was after this that their eyes were opened and they knew they were naked and had to sew fig leaves to make themselves coverings. It was then the voice of the Lord came walking in the garden. Of course, God knew what had happened, but he asked the question (verse 11) "Have you eaten of the tree from which I commanded you that you should not eat?"

Adam's reply was to blame the woman, "The woman you gave to be with me she gave me of the tree and I ate" (verse 12).

When the Lord then asked the woman, "What is this you have done?"

She replied, "The serpent deceived me and I ate" (verse 13).

So Adam blamed his wife Eve, and she blamed the serpent! Human nature looks to project blame on someone else.

The prodigal could have gone down this road and blamed everyone else including the prostitutes or his so-called friends and the gambling dens, bars, and everything else that took his money. But projecting guilt away from himself would never have solved his problem. It simply leaves the person who chooses to do this, feeding pigs in the pigsty so to speak, and no reconnections with the people that really matter the most, family. No one helped him. He was left alone, but his next move was the all-important one.

Like the chess player who sits and studies the board considering his options, the prodigal had some serious thinking to do. One option was to stay where he was and suffer loneliness, working in the pigsty. The other was to come to terms with the truth and ownership of his sin! The latter calls for radical change, and the heart opened up for divine heart surgery. It is painful and humbling when a person is prepared to lay everything out in the open and own their actions, deeds, words, and sin. The alternative is to remain stuck in the mud of the pigsty and try and get used to loneliness! What appears to be the painful route actually is the one that leads to healing. All surgery is never very nice, but the patient doesn't stay in pain for the rest of their lives. Serious thinking was what was needed in order for the prodigal to come to terms with the truth that "there is always a way back."

Chapter 9

The Turning Point

I t is interesting to note the phrase "he came to himself," (Luke 15:16) another way of saying this would be "he came to his senses." It's sad but true, but it's only when some people hit rock bottom they realize there is only one way to go, and that's up, because they can't get any lower! This was exactly where the prodigal found himself, rock bottom! In the process of coming to his senses, his mind thought of the hired servants back at home that was better off than he was. He did a commonsense comparison; he was a son, and he was hungry, alone and in a pigsty with nowhere to call home. Sometimes it pays to talk to yourself especially if you are going to talk sense that will lead to the right decision. The book of Proverbs exhorts, "Do not eat the bread of a miser, nor his delicacies: for as he thinks in his heart so is he . . ." (Proverbs 23:6–7). The mind is very powerful; it is seat of all our thoughts; it is the harbor for many things both good and bad. It is the battlefield of the mind that every believer has to win if they are to experience real transformation. The Apostle Paul taught that transformation comes by the renewing of the mind. ". . . do not be conformed to this world but be transformed by the renewing of your mind, that you may prove what is that good and perfect will of God" (Romans 12:1–3) The believer has to apply the Word of God and its truths of who they are in Christ, e.g., the grace of God, forgiveness, their acceptance, and relationship with God (Ephesians 1). "Sons of God, heirs of the Father and joint heirs with Christ" (Romans 8:17) are some of the truths that when embraced by faith renew the mind from victim mentality, failure, and the feeling of unworthiness.

Paul also taught that in order to overcome all the negative thoughts that the devil loves to inflict upon the believers' mind, to combat these, there is a "helmet of salvation." The helmet protects the mind; it is one of the pieces of spiritual armor that Paul lists in Ephesians chapter 6. It basically means we have to feed our mind upon the salvation, new life, and deliverance that Christ gives when someone genuinely repents of their sin and receives Christ as Savior. Of course the opposite happens when our mind is filled with negative thoughts of fear and unbelief. Let me illustrate this from the life of David in the Old Testament. David was fleeing from King Saul who was filled with jealousy and bitterness against David who had slain Goliath. It was the fear that David was becoming more popular than he was, and Saul sought to slay the giant slayer! David was on the run; he was being hunted by Saul's army, hiding in caves. We find these words recorded in 1 Samuel 27:1, "And David said in his heart, 'Now I shall perish someday by the hand of Saul. There is nothing better for me than that I should speedily escape to the land of the Philistines: and Saul will despair of me, to seek me anymore in any part of Israel, so shall I escape out of His hand.'" This was one of David's grave mistakes and sins to escape to the enemies of Israel and to offer to fight alongside the armies of the giant he had killed! David totally backslid from the place of faith and operated in fear! This all took place because David had said in his heart, "Now I shall perish someday by the hand of Saul . . ." In other words, David was playing this over and over in his mind, so much so that it was translated into actions. He joined the ranks of the enemy army!

Falling moral standards are constantly on display through the media. This then infiltrates the human mind, and this in turn results in lifestyle behavior. What we see happening is simply the out workings of what is taking place in the thought patterns of the human mind! When God called Gideon to fight the Midianites (Judges 6:1–14), he was basically in hiding not sharpening his sword and planning battle strategies! The Midianites would come at the time of harvest and destroy Israel's food supply. When God sent an angel to speak to Gideon, the angel addressed him as a mighty man of valor. That was the furthest thing from Gideon's mind at that time. In his own mind and thoughts, he had never contemplated himself as a "mighty man of valor." It almost seemed like a joke if it hadn't have been so supernatural and real. What God was seeking to do was to implant in his mind how He saw Gideon and dispel the negative thought of how Gideon saw Gideon! Do you see the spiritual principle here? Before you can move from the place of defeat to victory, there has to be a "mind change."

Mind change only takes place when we want to break out of the mold that perhaps has been keeping us from our destiny. A mold is a hollow form or matrix giving a particular shape to something in a molten or plastic state. When clay is poured into a mold, once it is set, the mold can be removed, and the replica of the mold is now duplicated into clay. Behind the onslaught of falling morals and a world that has become prodigal in its standards and behavior is the enemy of souls the devil himself who has engineered a mold for the human mind. The Bible says he has blinded the minds of those who do not believe lest the light of the gospel of Christ should shine on them (2 Corinthians 4:4). He blinds the mind then seeks to fill the mold of the mind with lust, selfishness, pride, and everything else that will lead to a spiritually reckless life filled with extravagant sin. We may ask the question, why society is like it is today and why have standards of morality collapsed? The answer is that the mold of the human mind is being bombarded with the clay from hell which in turn produces spiritual prodigals. Some have lost their faith; others have never had any kind of faith in God and others as referred to earlier in the book who are spiritually deceived and in confusion. This in turn produces a world and society that swims with the current of godless living, and one day we will stand before God with the mud and mess of sin all over them! Then it will be too late to break the mold; it will be too late for turning toward home. It is right now at this moment the mold can be broken! In the business world, people use the term "think outside the box." In order to succeed in a competitive world, there has to be innovation, plans, and strategies that will take them out of the ordinary and break them into the world where the customer will take notice. Breaking free from the mold isn't always easy; it's challenging and demanding. We can so easily feel comfortable with the familiar, and to break from that is to step out of our comfort zones. But comfort doesn't provide challenges; it speaks of ease. For the prodigal, he was no longer in a "comfort zone"; he was in a pigsty. There was nothing comfortable about his present situation at all.

In financial recovery, the experts will tell you to take certain steps to put yourself on the road to recovery. The first step is to "accept your situation" and to stop wallowing in your misery and accept reality. You might be a victim of something someone else has done but as devastating as that may be, that will not change your situation. Don't live in the past or even try to resist what has happened. What has happened has happened; accept your situation. You can't turn the clock back; there is only one way to go, and that's forward. It is figuring out the plan and strategy forward; that is all important. For the prodigal, this was exactly where he was; he had accepted his situation with much reluctance. Never in his wildest dreams did he believe he would be walking through pig's dung and working in that environment each day! That was where he was, but he came to his senses, assessed his situation, and thought about what was happening back home. When he came to his senses, he saw himself as he really was. There was no one else to blame for the mess he was in but him! His sin had caught up with him, and God who has watched and seen everything in His love and passion to rescue and restore had been at work behind the scenes with the famine. This same god was now opening this young man's eyes to see what the real state of his heart was like. The Psalmist David cried out to the Lord when confronted with his sin "... my sin is always before me. Against You, You only have I sinned, and done this evil in your sight" (Psalm 51:4). When the Holy Spirit draws back the curtain of the human heart, what is on stage is not always good viewing! Jeremiah the prophet wrote, "The heart is deceitful above all things and desperately wicked, who can know it? (Jeremiah 17:9). The truth is God knows it, and for the prodigal, this was the moment he looked into his own heart and saw his sin. This was the moment he had to own it; he couldn't shift the blame to anyone else, but to return home wouldn't be easy, and he had no idea how he would be received. He started his journey although a long way from home, a journey that would lead him to the truth that "there is always a way back."

Chapter 10

The Path of Humility

The prodigal was a long way from home, but he was the one who had chosen to live in a country that was a great distance from his father's house. The journey home looked daunting; his home country seemed almost unreachable. There was no quick stride in his steps as there was when he first stepped out from his father's house, on what he thought would be a great adventure. The prodigal gathered together what little he had, clasped his one bag in his hand, and started on the journey home. A journey that would probably take him many weeks, with long exhausting days and sleeping rough at night, unless by some fortune he could hitch a ride along the way. His first steps, as he left the pigsty behind, seemed as though there was lead in his boots. But with the stench of the pigsty still lingering on his clothes, he started the long trek home. He looked a pitiful figure making his way down the long winding dirt road; his head bowed low, as each step he took he contemplated all that had transpired over the time spent away from his father's house. The figure walking down the road that day was a young man who seemed to have the weight of the world on his shoulders. He played over and over in his mind the utter sin that he had allowed himself to become a servant to. This indeed was the path of humility. He had left home as a young man who wouldn't listen to fatherly advice. Pride would not allow him to listen! He thought he knew it all and could handle anything in the new life he sought. But now pride was dead and buried in the mud of the pigsty he had left behind.

The path of humility is something our selfish carnal nature will resist vehemently. But for the prodigal, it was the only way home, and it is the same path for every prodigal; it's the same path for me and for you.

The story is told of two mountain goats. High upon a narrow path the two goats faced each other. Each wanted to go in the opposite direction. They stared at each other and tried to pass, but there was no room, and one would certainly be pushed over the side to probable death. They butted heads for a while but got nowhere, until one lay down and let the other walk over him. The problem was solved; each goat could then carry on its journey. Neither would have got to where they wanted to go, unless one had laid down and humbled himself. For the one goat, it would be a little painful and humiliating, but it was needful.

I remind you of a verse mentioned earlier in the book when God gave specific instructions to King Solomon regarding the nation of Israel. If they backslid from following the Lord and allowed idolatry and other practices to take the place of their worship of the most high, there was a way back. It is found in 2 Chronicles 7:14, "If My people who are called by my name will humble themselves and pray and seek my face, and turn from their wicked ways then will I hear from heaven, and forgive their sin, and heal their land." God's people had to humble themselves! This was the key; this was the way back to God's blessing and God's healing of their land. To humble ourselves before the Lord is to admit we don't deserve His blessing and favor. The Bible teaches that God resists the proud and gives grace to the humble (James 4:6). We may fast, pray, shout, or do whatever we may think will get God's attention, but unless there is humility, He will resist the proud. Pride was the sin that caused Satan to rebel from the high and lofty position of being the anointed cherub (Isaiah 14). Pride walks hand in hand with selfishness; it lifts the heart to a place where it cannot be taught and corrected and shirks submission. The turning point for the prodigal was a change of mind. The mind-set of pride had been broken by his dire need. The very thing that started him on the journey home was the "change of mind" which was the turning point.

This is what the Bible actually calls "repentance"; it primarily means a change of mind. The common deception of earning favor with God and a place in heaven, by "good works," smacks of pride. It is basically saying in the face of God, "You may have sent your Son to die, but I didn't need His sacrifice. I'm good enough!" That's offensive to God who so loved us that He gave His only begotten Son that whoever believes in Him should not perish but have eternal life (John 3:16). Pride causes men and women to walk by the cross and look the other way! It is the exaltation of self and a blockade to the blessing and favor of God. As the Lord watched the prodigal take those first few steps, heaven must have smiled. It was like dawn breaking over the long dark winter night. Angels must have watched with great interest as God taught them again the truth that "there is always a way back." The frozen soil compacted by snow, the bare trees bereft of leaves, and the perennial flowers that disappeared as winter struck all await the miracle of spring. This was what was happening in the prodigal's heart. A new day was about to dawn, but first he has to make the journey.

Have you ever felt like giving up on a long walk or journey? If the desired destination is worth the effort, you may rest for a while but never give up! My two sons, Mark and Paul, ran the marathon, and both were raising money for Africa. Mark was raising money for an agriculture tractor we were planning to buy for a little village in Uganda called Kapyani, and Paul and his wife Melissa were raising money for water for Africa with "World Vision." Each said the same thing the last few miles were the hardest. That is where determination and perseverance have to win through, to get you to the finishing line! I tell this story although I have never run a marathon myself; I thought I was doing well completing the 5K. (I do have a medal to prove it!)

You are now part way through the book. Please keep reading as the best is yet to come!

The prodigal was now on the road of humility which is easy to give up. The temptation is always there when the legs get weary.

When walking on the road of humility, pride is always lurking around the corner to take you offtrack. I remember hearing the story of a young man who was a new convert to Christianity, asking his pastor one day if he could help him overcome "pride." The pastor told him that he had the very thing that would help him to get rid of all pride. He pointed him to a sandwich board which was in a storeroom in the church. On one side it read, "Repent, the coming of the Lord is nigh," and on the other, "Be sure your sin will find you out." The pastor told him to go to the market square and stand there for several hours with this board over his shoulders. The young man was excited to do this, and off he went carrying the sandwich board to the town center. He stood there with face gleaming, until a group of school children came by laughing and throwing some rotten tomatoes at the board. Adults jeered some spat and shouted abuse. After a few hours, it was a rather dejected young man that made his way back to the church. The pastor greeted him, but the young man could hardly lift up his head and make eye contact. He slowly placed the board down in the storeroom. It was then the pastor congratulated him and said, "Not many people would have done what you have done today." When the young man heard that, he quickly lifted his head, looked straight at the pastor, and said with great pride, "Really?" Pride can quickly retake its place on the throne of the human heart when compliments are paid, if we are not careful.

Pride is the enemy of repentance and the author of rebellion. Pride never wants to admit wrong. It always wants to be in control. It is the enemy of spiritual growth, the very thing that aborts prayer and brings a divide between man and God. I am sure we can all remember when we were kids and parents wanted us to take medicine that wasn't very nice tasting. Usually, children will grimace, close their eyes, and swallow as quickly as possible. That's after much resistance and a lot of persuasion and bribery, with a promise of something tasting much better. I can still hear the words, "It will make you better. Swallow it." Swallowing wasn't easy, but it was worth it, although at the time, I was not too sure. We have all heard the saying "swallow your pride." Swallowing our pride doesn't taste very good either. As the prodigal set off on his journey home, he had to take several big gulps to swallow his pride and convince himself that what he was about to do would be worth it in the long run. As human beings, we are constantly dogged with the temptation to harbor pride. It's not always visible; it can hide in the human heart, but it's real, and it's an enemy of humility.

Think for a moment of the Lord of Glory, the god who created all things by the Word of His power (Hebrews 1:3). This same god is described as having this world as a footstool (Isaiah 66:1). The Prophet Habakkuk described the power of God in terms like this— "His brightness was like the light. He had rays flashing from His hand, and there His power was hidden . . . He stood and measured the earth; He looked and startled the nations, and the everlasting mountains were scattered, the perpetual hills bowed. His ways are everlasting . . ." (Habakkuk 3:4, 6). Did you notice the phrase (verse 4) "and there His power was hidden"? The prophet was simply writing not of the display of the power of God but of God hiding His power! If you hide something, you put it out of sight. The prophet, when describing what we would think are displays of the power of God, is actually saying that these are not displays of His power. His awesome power is hidden and not yet on view! Yet it is this same god who humbled Himself to come in the form of a man and eventually even to the death on the cross (Philippians 2:5–11). Paul uses this as an example and in the opening verses of that same chapter, encourages the Christians at Philippi to do nothing through selfish ambition or conceit, but in lowliness of mind to esteem each other better than himself (verse 3). Think for a moment of some of the things Jesus said and taught which show us His humility and His obedience to his Father.

"The Son can do nothing of Himself" (John 5:19).

"I seek not my own glory . . ." (John 8:50).

"Learn of Me, for I am lowly of heart" (Matthew 11:29).

"Whosoever will be chief among you, let him be your servant, even as the Son of Man came to serve" (Matthew 20:27).

Perhaps one of the greatest example of Christ's humility was when He took the bowl and towel and washed His disciple's feet (John 13). This was just prior to the Passover, and Jesus knew He was soon to be betrayed and go through the torture of the Roman whipping post and then to death upon the cross. He actually washed the feet of Judas, His betrayer! If we dare to meditate upon these things, what right have we to harbor any pride at all!

The great chapter on "love" recorded in 1 Corinthians 13 affirms the truth that there is no pride in love; real love has humility at its root. Pride should be resisted at all costs while we live in this earthly body. As we are allowed to look briefly at worship in heaven, we find no trace of it there at all, rather the opposite. The multitudes of believers (thankful to God for His great sacrifice and the blood of Jesus that paid the ultimate price for their salvation) are filled with words such as "blessings and honor, glory and power, be to Him who sits on the throne and to the Lamb, forever and ever." This is the kind of worship that fills the courts of heaven. There is no trace of pride! (Revelation 5:13–14)

I was listening to the preacher David Jeremiah on TV, and he gave a humorous illustration of how grandkids have a way of bringing us back to a place of humility. He told the story of the day after President Donald Trump's inauguration; he was invited with a number of other well-known preachers to take part in prayer service in Washington DC. I remember watching this on TV and wondering what had happened to David Jeremiah as he went to the pulpit to read a portion of scripture from the book of Romans. He seemed to take ages to find the scripture. In relating this story, several months later in his TV message, he told his congregation that there was a sheet of paper with all the different readings on that each preacher in turn would read. When he got to the pulpit (and remember millions were watching on TV), he discovered the previous preacher had taken the paper with him as he went back to his seat. David Jeremiah was first of looking for this paper and then had to leave the pulpit and borrow a Bible from a friend sitting close by. When he got back to the pulpit, realizing this had taken some time, he said his fingers felt like they were twice the size as he was so nervous and conscious of the time he was taking. He eventually found the book of Romans and read the portion. When he eventually arrived home, his little granddaughter said to him, "Grandpa, I saw you on TV reading from the Bible," he was so pleased she had taken interest, but then she said, "But, Grandpa, it took you a long time to find the book of Romans. Didn't you know where it was?"

The fact that the prodigal was on his way home was the most important thing; repentance and humility always lead to action. He had turned his back on the pigsty and on a life of sin and excessive wasteful living. He had discovered, as hard as it may seem, "there is always a way back."

Chapter 11

What Had His Father Been Doing?

It is an interesting thought "what had his father been doing all the time his son was away?" We are not actually told what he had been doing in the story. But we can surmise from the fact that his father had the best robe, a ring, and sandals all prepared, along with a fatted calf just ready to be slaughtered for a welcome home meal.

Allow me to remind you that our heavenly Father had been watching and working behind the scenes and had allowed the prodigal to experience a famine which really brought him to his knees. When need takes over from want, that is the call for action. This is exactly what had happened.

Back at home I think there were several things that had been taking place, the kind of things that become a habit and overwhelming for any concerned parent whose son or daughter decide on reckless and wasteful living. The first thing to mention is that he had been patiently waiting for the day when his son would return. It is only the parents that have gone through the mental torture of wondering what and where their son or daughter is and what they are doing that can empathize with the prodigal's father. Each day that dawned, he peered through the window looking for his boy. Would this be the day? Would this day bring the moment he had been waiting for? As the father went about his daily work on the little farm, there were times I'm sure when his thoughts were far away and at times even when spoken to he seemed distant. The fact was he was consumed with other things. The farm and everything that was needed to keep it going and functioning was important of course, but not as important as the one thing that consumed his thoughts, his son.

For a parent, it is a testing time. It's a time in one sense of feeling helpless, and in another way of leaning on the faithfulness of God, being reminded of God's promises and at the same time resisting every negative thought that the devil tries to inflict upon the mind. It's a totally different experience for parents when the child comes of age and parental restraints can be discarded. I think the prodigal's father had a heart that was desperately waiting and hoping for the day when his son would return. Not only would he be waiting, but like any believing parent, he would have been praying. I remember a minister friend relating the story of his teenage daughter. She had not left home but had backslid in her heart. She was still at school but had lost interest in spiritual things. Her bedroom walls were filled with pictures of a certain rock group of the day whose songs portrayed an opposite lifestyle to the way she had been taught. Her dad would walk around her bedroom each day while she was at school and pray, also reminding the devil this was one less day she would be under his grip and influence. The day came when his daughter came back to the Lord and today she is serving the Lord and married to a pastor.

Nothing tests our faith more than when our children are in need of a miracle of grace in their life. As each day dawned, I can imagine as the sun was dawning upon the little farmhouse, the father would be sitting on his porch, his heart reaching out to God in faith for a son he had not heard of, or seen, in many days. Tears would often stream down his face when he raised his heart to God. This was not a chore; it was a necessity and had become a way of life. This was his prayer! I am reminded of the time when an angel came to Zechariah the husband of Elizabeth and said, "Your prayer has been heard and your wife Elizabeth will bear you a son and you shall call his name John" (Luke 1:11–19). Both Zechariah and Elizabeth were not young. These are people whom the Bible describes as being well advanced in years. For the angel to tell them their prayer had been heard is indicative of the fact that they basically had one prayer they prayed daily. It was a prayer that they breathed out, sometimes in sighs and tears, but it was their one main prayer. His prayer the angel said had been heard.

It is quite challenging to ask ourselves if an angel appeared to us and said the same thing as he did to Zechariah; what would that prayer be? Is there one main prayer that perhaps you have been praying for years, and as of now you haven't seen the answer? Perhaps if you are a parent or grandparent and you have been praying for a prodigal son or daughter, don't give up; your prayers have been heard. Daniel kept praying although his prayer was heard from the first day he commenced. It was twenty-one days later that the answer came (Daniel 10). The problem so often is having the answers come back to earth, that is, where spiritual battles take place and the enemy of our souls seeks to resist every prodigal from returning to the Father's blessing. In Exodus 17:8–16, we have the story of Amalek who came to fight against Israel. Moses stood on the hill as the battle raged below. As Aaron and Hur lifted up the hands of Moses, Israel prevailed. As his hands were let down, Amalek prevailed, but Aaron and Hur brought a stone for Moses to sit on and continued to support his hands steady until the sun went down. As a result, Israel prevailed, and the battle was won. Let me encourage everyone to believe that God hears and is working behind the scenes. Keep lifting up your prayers to God. He is at work. There may be times in this spiritual battle when you feel weary; those are the times when we can call for support in prayer, join forces, and press through to victory.

Just recently, my wife and I were staying at the Starved Rock Lodge in Illinois. It is a beautiful state park with lovely walks and high rocky hills. It is situated along the Illinois River less than one hundred miles from Chicago. Native Americans, called the Archaic Indians, were the first inhabitants. According to Native American tradition in the 1760s, Chief Pontiac of the Ottawa tribe was attending a tribal council meeting. The head chief of the Illinois tribe stabbed Chief Pontiac. Vengeance arose in Pontiac's followers. A battle ensued, and the Illinois, fearing death, took refuge on the great rock. After many days, the remaining Illinois died of starvation giving the historic park its name—Starved Rock.

We were just returning from a walk when we met two couples who were about to ascend the same 280 steps back up to the lodge. They asked us where we were from originally, having detected a difference in our accent, and we enjoyed a conversation as we made our way back to the lodge. That night, after dinner, they asked us to join them in the lounge. One of the men assured us that he was no longer a believer. He had been brought up as a Catholic but had been convinced in his younger days that there was no truth in Christianity. We were able to share our stories of how both Val and I had come to know the Lord and some of the miracles we had seen over the years. The gentleman, who had assured us he was no longer a believer, then said something very interesting. He told us that his sister was a firm believer in Jesus Christ and prayed for him every day! I assured him we would also pray for him.

I include this story to encourage all who are praying for prodigals. God has His missionaries all over the place, and He can orchestrate meetings that are not by chance at all but are divine encounters to speak to prodigals. We left them that evening just believing this wasn't a coincidence but God arranged it. We were able to sow and water some gospel seed into their lives, and one day, we trust we will meet again, if not in this world then in heaven.

A young man called me one hot summer day and asked if he could talk to me about his business. He had pulled my name out of the local chamber of commerce directory. We arranged to meet at the local Starbucks coffee shop. We had been speaking just a short while when he asked the question as to where I was from; once again my accent had given away the fact that I wasn't an American. It does lead to some interesting conversations at times! When I told him I was the pastor of a local church in the town, he immediately said that his girlfriend was a Christian and so was his boss at work and that both were praying for him. We never really got down to the business he had initially wanted to talk about; he just kept asking me questions about Christianity. This went on for about two hours, and we arranged to meet later in the afternoon this time at another venue "Panera Bread." We sat outside in the summer sun, and the conversation continued where we had left off. After about another hour or more of explaining the way of salvation and the great sacrifice Jesus had paid upon the cross, I asked him if he really wanted to give his life over to the Lord Jesus. There was no hesitation on his part. Under the umbrella of one of the little tables, with our coffee cups now empty but still on the table, he prayed a simple but sincere prayer for salvation. I can only imagine the joy of his girlfriend and his boss when he told them the news! Prayers do get answered, and God is at work. Take heart praying parents or whoever you are. Nothing gets missed by a loving heavenly Father. Months later the next time I saw this young man, he told me he was regularly attending a church with his girlfriend and had just returned from a mission trip to Brazil!

I remember years ago reading Jim Cymbala's book, *Fresh Wind, Fresh Fire*. Jim is pastor of a great church, the Brooklyn Tabernacle. In the book, he relates the story of his daughter Chrissy, who at eighteen years of age decided to go her own way. He found that very difficult as any caring parent would. She went right away from the Lord, left the family home, and left both Jim and his wife in tears. The scripture came to him one day, "Call upon Me in the day of trouble and I will answer you." He relates how he dissolved in a flood of tears but knew he had to let go of the situation. He prayed with intensity, interceding, and praising God for what he knew God would do soon. Christmas came and went but no Chrissy. One cold winter night in February at the Tuesday night prayer gathering, the church heard him talk from Acts chapter 4 and how the early church lifted up their voice in one accord. A note was handed to him from a young woman in the church who felt they should all pray and intercede for Chrissy. I found his next description very interesting! The church turned into a labor room! The Apostle Paul wrote to the Galatian church and told them he was laboring again in the pains of childbirth for Christ to be formed in them (Galatians 4:19). When Jim got home that night, he had this very real sense that "it was over"; something had happened God had intervened.

It was the next morning as he was upstairs shaving that he heard his wife Carol shout, "Chrissy is here!"

He went downstairs to see Chrissy on her knees sobbing on the kitchen floor.

In anguish, she cried out, "Daddy! Daddy! I've sinned against you and mommy. Please forgive me." That was the day when Chrissy discovered "there is always a way back." She then asked who was praying for her on Tuesday night, because that night God had given her a dream of the abyss she was heading toward but that God was wrapping His arms around her saving her from sliding into it.

Take heart praying, friend. God is always at work! I had the privilege just a year ago of listening to Chrissy's story at a local conference Val and I were attending. She is now married, and along with her husband, they pastor Chicago Tabernacle. It's a great church, and shortly after that conference, we took a group from our church to their Tuesday evening prayer service; hundreds were in attendance, praying for souls to be saved and prodigals to return home.

What had the Father been doing in the story Jesus told? He most certainly had been praying. I'm sure also that the father in the story had not simply been waiting and praying, but he had been preparing." Preparing for the day when his son would return. He had the best robe waiting hanging in his closet, clean, ironed, and ready to be worn. Each day as the father reached into his closet for his own garments, he would see this robe. I can imagine in a modern-day setting it would be hung up protected in a plastic cover, but occupying a special place in that closet, set apart from all the other garments. This one had reserved tagged on it; it was waiting for the day when the coat hanger would be removed and it would be placed upon the returned prodigal. There was one drawer that had one special item that was also waiting for the son's return; it was a ring. This was reserved also along with a pair of sandals. The father must have said to himself many times that when his son returned, he would be treated like a son, not a peasant or servant. The father had not just been praying; he had been preparing for the day that would be like no other day.

I imagine that he prayed a day would dawn that would erase all the horrid memories of when his son walked out and left his home. This is what the father lived for, and this is what he believed for, to patiently wait and prepare speaks of faith. He definitely had faith. None of the other things are to any avail without it, but when you have it, the other things simply follow on. Faith is a verb. It's a doing word; it's action; it is never complacent. The writer of the book of Hebrews (11:1) tells us, "Now faith is the substance of things hoped for the evidence of things not seen." Think about this for a moment. Everything we make needs substance. You can't make a wooden table without first of all having wood. A baker can't make cakes without the proper ingredients. Everything we see and use has to have substance. Faith is the substance of what we hope for or what we are praying for. As verse 3 states, even the worlds (universe) were framed by the Word of God, the Word being the substance! "Without faith it is impossible to please God for he who comes to God must believe that He is and that He is a rewarder of those who diligently seek Him" (verse 6). Faith then is the title deed, the assurance of what we are praying for. A title deed cannot be argued against; it speaks of ownership. Everything the father had prepared spoke of the fact that he had the title deed of his son's return. Faith then as already stated is a "verb." To read through Hebrews 11 is to be confronted with action faith, Abel offering his sacrifice, Noah preparing an ark, Abraham obeying God, and Moses forsaking Egypt and obeying the commission of God. Faith always moves the believer to action, even if the action is a patient waiting for the answer.

The one thing I have not yet mentioned in the father's preparation was "the fatted calf!" I remember visiting a minister friend who was brought up on his father's farm. He invited us over to the farm for a BBQ. The steaks were sizzling on the grill. These were not burgers that had just been defrosted; these were real "man-sized steaks." I commented on the size of them. He told me that he had been stroking this calf for many months and fattening him up! We laughed at the thought that he had been thinking about the steak even when the creature roamed in the field. But this is what I believe the father had been doing too.

Keep believing, prepare, and be ready for the day. God is at work even now as you read this book. A new dawn will break because the Holy Spirit will do the work only He can do, and He is in the business of revealing the truth that "there is always a way back."

Chapter 12

When the Father Runs

How long it took the prodigal to get home? I don't know. How many miles did he walk? I can only surmise that it could have taken weeks as he had gone "into a far country." Maybe he could have hitched a ride with some passerby, although he was probably looking bedraggled and weary, and many I'm sure would have passed him by. Maybe perhaps one would have taken pity and offered him a ride for at least part of the journey. Let's imagine that happened and he still had some twenty miles or more to walk to finally arrive at home, humbled, weary, and with a completely different state of mind to the one he left with. Now the only thoughts that filled his mind are recorded in Luke15:18–19, "I will arise and go to my father and will say to him, 'Father I have sinned against heaven and before you, and I am no longer worthy to be called your son. Make me like one of your hired servants.'" These words were rehearsed time and again as the prodigal took each step on his long journey. Pride had left him in the pigsty; now there was no trace of it all. Life has a habit of doing just that! The prodigal didn't need anyone to convince him of his sin and wayward life; circumstances under the control of a loving god had brought him to his knees. It is interesting to note that he first acknowledged his sin that was against heaven and then before his father also.

Allow me to take you back to one of the great characters in the Old Testament, namely, David, the young man who was the giant killer, who became so popular that Saul the ing wanted him killed. David, the fugitive, eventually became king just as Samuel the prophet had said. He rose from being hunted like a criminal to the throne of Israel. This mighty warrior was not with his fighting troops this particular time. He was on his housetop in the cool of the evening (2 Samuel 11). From his rooftop, he saw a woman bathing, and the woman was very beautiful to behold (verse 2). David could have looked away at that moment, but he didn't. He allowed lust to ferment in his heart so much, so when he made inquiries as to who she was, he discovered she was the wife of Uriah the Hittite, one of his own fighting warriors. David was the king. He had come a long way and through many hardships, trials, and life lessons to the place where he was now, in a place of power and authority. The problem is that "power" can corrupt, yet it is the one thing many strive for. World wars have been started because the lust of power has been the driving force, even if it meant death to millions!

David was now in the powerful position as king. He had swallowed the lie and deception that what he wanted he could have, even if that meant someone else's wife! David sent messengers and took her (verse 4)! It gives the impression that there was no debate and no reasoning or persuading. He simply took her like a thief stealing someone's property. He didn't take long, and once she was brought to his residence, adultery took place. This is because he had already "taken her" in his heart. Bathsheba became pregnant, the king was informed, and he had to conceive a plan to cover it all up. But sin can never be covered up! The Father sees everything. David's plan was to make sure her husband was thrown into the front line of battle so he would be killed. This is exactly what had happened, and David took Bathsheba to his own house, and everything seemed to be covered up. But God had other ideas. He wasn't finished with David, and neither was He going to let David get away with his sin.

Nathan the prophet came to the king one day and told him a story (2 Samuel 12). It was the story of two men in one city, one poor and the other rich. The rich man had many flocks, but the poor man only had one little ewe lamb, which was the family pet. A traveler came to visit the rich man, but the rich man wouldn't take one of his own lambs to make a meal for his guest. Instead, he took the only ewe lamb the poor man had. David could not restrain himself from an outburst of anger and immediately said to Nathan the prophet the rich man must be put to death, and he must first restore four times as much as he took!

The net had been spread, and David walked right into it! "As the Lord lives," said David. Imagine David brought the name of the Lord into the whole scenario! He was so deceived by his own sin. The giant killer had now been slain by another giant called deception.

No sooner had these words left David's mouth the prophet said, "You are the man!"

His sin was uncovered, out in the open; the words of the prophet that followed cut him deep within his heart. David's response was immediate (verse 13), "I have sinned against the Lord." This was one of the worst days of David's life, but the redeeming thing in all of this was David's immediate response—repentance! David, like the prodigal, immediately recognized he had sinned against the Lord. This was indeed the father running toward His prodigal king, running to rescue him. In order to rescue him, He had to uncover his sin. It was a clean heart that God was looking for. Although David had hidden his sin prior to Nathan's visit, he had struggled in his own conscience and heart (Psalm 51). In this Psalm of David, we are allowed into his inner heart and his struggles when he writes, "My sin is always before me, and against You, You only have I sinned and done this evil in your sight . . ." When the father runs, it is not always to receive the prodigal but to chase him down!

The day dawned like every other day in the long months since the prodigal left home. But I can imagine this particular day was a little different. As the father rose from his bed and prepared himself something to eat for breakfast, he couldn't explain it, but maybe he felt there was something different about this day. It was almost like God the Father was giving him the "heads-up" in his spirit, preparing him for one of God's special "suddenlies." It was God about to prove to the prodigal's father that He had been working behind the scenes and in fact He had been running and chasing down his wayward son. The story of the Bible is God running, so to speak, after the lost mankind. He is not willing that any should perish; that has never been the will of God. Calvary shows us in very clear terms the extreme love of God. This was not God just running but dying! This was the eternal all powerful, loving, holy God becoming man in order to provide a way back to Him. Way back in the garden of Eden, it was God who came looking for Adam. It was God who was calling out, "Adam where are you?" Adam was hiding; God was seeking him.

Since that time millions have hid behind their excuses, but that has never hindered or stopped God from running after them. He sent His Holy Spirit into the world for that very reason to convict of the sin of unbelief and to convince sinners that through faith and repentance, they can become righteous in the sight of God, because at Calvary, Satan was destroyed or rendered powerless by the death of Jesus Christ, to stop any repentant sinner from finding God's salvation despite what sins they may have committed (John 16:8–11). As sin escalated upon the earth, God raised up a man called Noah and for one hundred years pleaded for men to repent. With a visual aid of a huge boat being built called the ark, God was running after a sin-sick world through the voice of one man called Noah. Down the ages, God has always pleaded (run after) His creation. When God created a nation called Israel, He was intending to show the world His blessing upon a people who would honor Him as their king. Instead, Israel eventually wanted an earthly king, one of flesh and blood, and the Old Testament reveals the depths of sin they slipped into. But God was not for sitting back and just watching all this take place along with the destruction of the nation He had created. Instead, He raised up prophets, and over a period of several hundred years, holy men of God spoke as they were moved by the Holy Spirit. Their message was uncompromising, and they demanded honor and glory be given to the Lord most high. They were no nonsense preachers, often misunderstood and persecuted but relentless in their message which demanded God be given first place in their lives rather than tagged onto their own agendas. They denounced sin and spoke of impending judgment if repentance was not heeded. As scathing as their message seemed at times, this was God facing His people up with their sin that they might turn to Him. This was the Father running!

Through the death and resurrection of Christ, the New Testament church was brought to birth, and before ascending back to His Father, Jesus left a group of followers with specific instructions. After the infilling of the Holy Spirit, they were to become witnesses to the uttermost parts of the world. They were to run with the message, and in so doing, they would be running with the Father, for He had assured them He would never leave them or forsake them. The Apostle Paul called ministry in terms like this—"We are workers together with Him" (2 Corinthians 6:1) or co-workers or co-runners. Paul knew firsthand what it was to be overtaken by the god who runs. He had been arrested by God and overtaken on the road to Damascus. Conversion took place as he encountered the living God. After that, Paul became a runner for the Father. He ran, so to speak, from community to community and nation to nation. He was a marathon runner for Jesus, until the time he would face execution. The race he ran was costly. It cost him his life but saved many others. Nothing moved him from running with the will of God; he preached the necessity of dedication when running in a race.

The Message:

> You've all been to the stadium and seen the athletes race; one wins. Run to win. All good athletes train hard. They do it for a gold medal that tarnishes and fades. You're after one that's gold eternally. I don't know about you, but I'm running hard for the finish line. I'm giving it everything I've got. No sloppy living for me! I'm staying alert and in top condition. I'm not going to get caught napping, telling everybody else all about it and then missing out myself.
>
> (1 Corinthians 9:24–27)

I well remember the time when my youngest son Paul was taking part in the annual school sports day. He was about nine years of age, and the race he was in took the boys round one lap of the sports field. He was all geared up for this race as Val and I, along with my parents, stood ready to cheer him on. The whistle blew and the race started. The runners were about half way around the field, and Paul was just behind the two or three front runners, reserving some energy for the last few hundred yards, when he was tripped up accidentally by one of the other runners. He fell to the ground and obviously lost ground on the front runners. We were cheering him on as he picked himself up quickly and gave chase to the front runners. I ran toward the finish line urging him on as he passed each boy in turn that was in front of him. There was only one boy left in front of him who wasn't too far away from the finish, but Paul was quickly gaining ground. The finish line was now just yards away, but Paul although just about to pass the boy in front and take first place just couldn't make it in time! Imagine the disappointment he felt, yet for us, we were so proud that he kept running and would have surely won had the course been just a few yards longer. Hey, but this was school sports day not the Olympics!

I share this story to remind everyone on your way to the finish line, or home, never give up. For the prodigal, on his way back to his father, there would probably have been times when he was at least tempted to give up, wondering what kind of reception he would receive. To those who are runners for God, spreading His Word, the gospel, and those who are praying for prodigals to come home, keep running with Him in prayer and faith. Don't allow anything along the journey to stop you; even if something along the way has seemingly set you back, it's time to get back up and head for the finishing line. Your heavenly Father is cheering you on, watching, listening, and waiting with the prize—a prodigal is on his way home.

One of the most inspirational stories which illustrate compassion and commitment is the following. The former British 400-meter record holder Derek Redmond was at his peak when he lined up for the 400-meter semifinal in Barcelona in 1992. Here he relives the day that ended his career but made him an inspiration to millions.

> When I took my place on the starting blocks I felt good. For once I had no injuries, despite eight operations in four years, and I'd won the first two rounds without breaking sweat—including post-

ing the fastest time in the first round heats. I was confident when the gun went off I got off to a good start. I got into my stride running the first turn and I was feeling comfortable. Then I heard a popping sound. I kept on running for another two or three strides then I felt the pain. I thought I'd been shot, but recognized the agony. I'd pulled my hamstring before and the pain is excruciating: like someone shoving a hot knife into the back of your knee and twisting it. I grabbed the back of my leg, uttered a few expletives and hit the deck. I couldn't believe this was happening after all the training I'd put in. I looked around to see where the rest of the field was, and they had only 100m to go. I remember thinking if I got up I could still catch them and qualify. The pain was intense. I hobbled about 50m until I was at the 200m mark. Then I realized it was all over. I looked round and saw that everyone else had crossed the finishing line. But I don't like to give up at anything—not even an argument, as my wife will tell you—and I decided I was going to finish that race if it was the last race I ever did. All these doctors and officials were coming onto the track, trying to get me to stop but I was not having any of it. Then with about 100m to go, I became aware of someone else on the track. I didn't realize it was my dad, Jim, at first he said, "Derek, it's me, you don't need to do this." I just said, "Dad, I want to finish, get me back in the semi-final." He said, "OK. We started this thing together and now we'll finish it together." He managed to get me to stop trying to run and just walk and he kept repeating, "You're a champion, you've got nothing to prove."

Today I don't feel anger, just frustration. The footage has since been used in adverts by Visa, Nike and the International Olympic Committee—I don't go out of my way to watch it, but it isn't painful anymore. We hobbled over the finishing line with our arms round each other, just me and my Dad, the man I'm really close to, who's supported my athletics career since I was seven years old. I've since been told there was a standing ovation by the 65000 crowd, but nothing registered at the time. I was in tears and went off to the medical room to be looked at, and then I took the bus back to the Olympic village. My dream was over. In Seoul four years earlier I didn't even get to the start line because of an Achilles injury and had "DNS"—Did Not Start—next to my name. I didn't want them to write "DNF"— Did Not Finish—in Barcelona. When I saw my doctor he told me I'd never represent my country again. I felt like there'd been a death. I never raced again and I was angry for two years. Then one day I just thought: there are worse things than pulling a muscle in a race, and I just decided to get on with my life. If I hadn't pulled my hamstring that day I could have been an Olympic medalist, but I love the life I have now. I might not have been a motivational speaker or competed for my country at basketball, as I went on to do. And my dad wouldn't have been asked to carry the Olympic torch which was a huge honor for him.

(Derek Redmond)

Our heavenly Father always runs to welcome prodigals back home, and even in the most difficult and painful times if necessary, He will pick us up and carry us over to a new day. The popular poem entitled "Footprints in the Sand" is the story of the life of one individual who had a dream that he was walking along the beach with the Lord. Scenes of his life flashed across the sky. He noticed that for each scene, there were two sets of footprints in the sand. One belonged to him and the other to the Lord. When it came to the saddest parts of his life, he noticed only one set of footprints. He was troubled by this as he believed that the Lord had promised to be with him every step of his journey through life. When he questioned the Lord about the reason why there was only one set of footprints, the Lord answered him by saying, "My precious child, I love you and will never leave you." The Lord went to explain that the reason for only one set of footprints during those difficult sad periods of his life was simply because the footprints were the Lord's. He had carried him though those times.

I remember the time that my late father-in-law, Albert Vizard, who was born in Wigan, Lancashire, England, took me to the old market square in Wigan town center. The market square was typical of so many in England at that time; it was paved with cobbles, and each week market traders would assemble their goods for sale under little canopies. When not in use by the market traders, it was used sometimes for public gatherings of various kinds, one of which was an open-air gospel service regularly conducted by one of the local churches on Saturday evenings. Years before, Val's mother, Francis, was very committed in her Christian faith and each week would be there singing and witnessing for the Lord. Albert and Francis at this time didn't know each other apart from the fact that Albert would often come out of the local pub which was situated nearby and having had a few too many beers (to put it mildly) would heckle and try and disrupt the service. But the young woman Francis caught his eye, and he said within his heart, "I'm going to marry that young lady one day." It was on one of those Saturday evenings that the Spirit of the Lord got hold of his heart as he heard the Word of God, and he knelt down in the market square and prayed that the Lord would forgive and save him. He actually took me to the exact spot and pointed to the cobble where he knelt and was saved. Eventually, he and Francis were married, but like so many at that time in England's history, as war broke out, he was called up to serve his country. It was while he was away that his faith began to slide and due also to the fact that there was not the support of a local church. Albert became a prodigal to the faith, and his drinking habits got the better of him. When he eventually returned home, his second home became the local pub. His weekly wages from his employment were mainly dwindled away on drink, and he would often be found staggering his way home, unable at times to even get his key in the front door of the house in order to unlock it and get in. Their home at that time was quite poor due to his drinking habits and his way of life.

Francis remained true to the Lord and was praying for him as well as continuing to attend her local church. Her pastor at that time was a man called George Deakin. It was George who took on the role of becoming "God's runner." He would visit Albert on a weekly basis and would always pray for him before leaving his home. George became the instrument God used, the one who portrayed God the Father as a runner, always ready to run toward a returning prodigal. He led Albert back to the Lord and to a complete restoration of faith. His drinking habits ceased, and his testimony was such that just as Jesus turned water into wine at the wedding in Galilee, in his home Jesus turned wine into furniture! The local pub no longer claimed the majority of his wage packet; it was used to furnish the home. Albert later became a pastor and planted a church in a nearby town called Leigh where he ministered for many years prior to his death. He also became one of God's runners always ready to share his story of conversion with anyone who would listen.

Just recently I heard of one such story that I found very interesting and encouraging. My brother-in-law Barry used to have a small hardware shop in Wigan. His parents Albert and Francis were visiting him on one particular day and were sitting in a storeroom at the back of the shop when a young man walked in. Barry went to serve him, and after the young man had paid for his goods and was about leave the shop, Albert felt constrained to talk to him and share his story with him. Before the young man left, Albert handed him a little gospel tract which explained the way of salvation. This took place well over twenty years ago. At the time of writing, my father-in-law has been dead some twenty-one years. What I am about to tell you is he had no idea what had happened. Several months ago, this same young man, who had never seen my brother-in-law Barry since that time, happened to meet him again in a local supermarket. One of the first things he told Barry was what happened that day after he had left his shop. He had kept that little tract and sometime later picked it up again and read it. The Holy Spirit so worked upon this young man's heart that he went along to a local church and heard the gospel again and was wonderfully saved. He went and shared his newfound faith with his father and family, and they had all come to know the Lord and had been baptized in water. My father-in-law knew nothing of what would transpire from that conversation with that young man that day, but I believe he will one day! Yes, one day all God's runners will meet the people they have helped along the journey to "home." There will be many surprises in heaven, along with great joy, praise, and thanksgiving because heaven will be much better than we have ever imagined!

Allow me one more story of a runner for God. This runner was a little old lady who has since, I'm sure, gone home to be with the Lord and receive her reward, but even in old age, she was a runner for God. First let me share about another elderly lady who is a marathon runner.

Just last year on the national news, it featured an old lady who was well into her late eighties who started to jog and train for the marathon (26 miles), when she had turned seventy years of age. She has since that time completed seventeen marathons. I share this to encourage everyone especially those who perhaps have slowed up in their witnessing for the Lord or have given up due to old age. God has His spiritual runners of all ages, and old age should never interfere with being a runner for God. Start jogging again and before too long, you will be running again for God.

With that said, I now return to the story that has always been an encouragement to me in more ways than one. When Val and I were living in the UK and were pastors of our first church in the town of Ulverston in Cumbria, we were busily engaged in seeking to grow the church in this lovely little market town. The Lord had helped us wonderfully in the planting of this new church, and people were coming to know the Lord and witnessing for Him. One of the couples in our church met another couple during the course of their business, who actually only lived several houses away from us in the next street. Their names are Viv and Jean Penfold. It was shortly after this that they were instrumental in Viv and his wife Jean coming to know the Lord as they visited with them in their home. Viv and Jean, along with their daughters, started attending our church.

I know there is a growing emphasis these days on discipleship which is very much needed, but all I can say regarding Viv and Jean is that they were the kind of converts every pastor dreams of. They had a desire to learn and an eagerness to become disciples. Within two years, Viv came into full-time ministry with us as an evangelist. We have been great friends over the years, and he has gone on to do a great work in India with discipleship and overseeing the planting of many churches as he has made the trip from the UK to India multiple times. Viv immediately became a runner for God, zealous to bring others to Christ, and particularly his parents, who lived at the other end of the country in Cornwall. I remember so well the times he would tell me that he had called them on the phone and witnessed to them, but they weren't particularly interested in hearing about the gospel. In fact, his dad was a little suspect of what his son was getting himself into. Some months later, Viv's parents, Len and Nellie, made the journey by train, some four hundred miles or more to check out our church. At the time of their visit, we were meeting in the local high school auditorium, while work on refurbishing a property we had purchased in the center of town was underway, for what would become our church meeting place and a Christian center. Len and Nellie sat through the meeting, and we were so glad to see them, because for months we had all been praying for them.

It was the following day when they were to board the train to return to Cornwall that Len turned to him as he was about to step onto the train, and his parting words were, "Son, don't let this religion rule your life!" We have laughed about this on many occasions since. However, this didn't deter Viv and Jean from praying and from weekly phone calls sharing what was happening at the church and how God was blessing them. Months past and then one day, we heard that Len and Nellie had bought a Bible! Wow we thought, *this is great news. God has them on His radar!* They also started to attend a local Anglican church near to where they lived. This news was greeted by more prayer and faith that they would soon become Christians themselves.

Now here is where I introduce you to the little old lady (God's runner). Len and Nellie decided to take another train journey, but this time to the city of London. They had been visiting some relatives for a few days and when boarding the train to return to Cornwall sat in one of the carriages, which would seat probably around six people, but this particular carriage was empty, so they put their cases on the rack and settled down for the journey. Just prior to the train leaving the station, an old lady boarded, preceded by her son who was carrying her cases. Her son walked by the carriage compartment where Len and Nellie were sitting and proceeded to walk further up the corridor perhaps looking for an empty carriage. As the old lady walked by the carriage where Len and Nellie were sitting, she shouted to her son, "Jesus wants me to sit here!" Her son turned back and helped his mother into the carriage, putting her case on the rack; he then kissed her goodbye and left her. As the train began to pull away from the station, Len was mulling over in his mind what the old lady had shouted to her son.

His curiosity got the better of him, and he couldn't resist asking the old lady, "What did you say to your son when you got to our carriage?"

She promptly replied without a second thought or any embarrassment, "I believe Jesus wanted me to sit here."

On hearing this, Len was now more curious as to why she would say that, so he began asking her question after question. And for the next several hours until the old lady reached her destination, he asked her about the Bible and salvation. She was the widow of a former pastor, and she was only too pleased to answer all his questions, because she was one of God's runners!

He never met that old lady again, but it was shortly after this that Viv received a phone call, from his parents with the news that they had both given their lives over to the Lord and had been wonderfully saved. We all rejoiced with them at the news, knowing this was a tremendous answer to prayer. Some time elapsed, but eventually another train journey took place, but this time Len and Nellie were moving to Ulverston, and Len eventually became our church treasurer. He helped us so much, guiding us through our building program, with his business background. I mentioned that Len and Nellie never saw the old lady again, at least on this earth, but now all are in heaven, and I'm sure they have thanked the little old lady for being sensitive to the Holy Spirit's voice and guidance that day on the train and for her willingness to be obedient and sit in their carriage. She did all of that simply because she was one of God's runners!

God has always had His runners; some men and women who down the centuries have left the security of their homeland to run with the torch of the gospel to foreign fields, forsaking their comfort zones, because a greater calling and destiny beckoned them. Others have served God in their local communities, but all have been runners for the Lord. They caught a vision and received a passion, and their life was no longer their own but belonged to the one who had given His life for them. God's runners are all over the world; in nations where the gospel is not allowed to be propagated, they still hold the torch. In a modern world, the tools for spreading the good news are immense with TV, Internet, and all the modern technology. The message spreads, and God chases and runs to embrace the prodigal sons and daughters calling them and cheering them home. This is and always has been the father's heart.

The Father always runs. The prodigal's father was a perfect example of our heavenly Father. This was the truth Jesus was seeking to teach. He was illustrating His heavenly Father's character. It was Jesus saying, "This is what My Father does." Imagine the prodigal as he got within sight of the little farmhouse he had called home for so many years. His heart was pounding and his mind rehearsing what he is going to say to his father. His head was bowed low as he looked at his worn dusty sandals that had by this time many miles of wear written all over them. The beads of sweat on his brow felt almost feverishly cold as his nerves began to get the better of him, and his hands began to shake and tremble. And with his heart pounding in his chest for a glimpsing moment, he dared to lift his head to look toward home. His eyes squinted in the sunlight and were glazed with tears, but he kept staring, wondering if his mind was playing tricks on him. He had thought he had seen the door opening. He stopped in his tracks as he realized this was not a trick of his imagination, because in the doorway stood a figure with his hands shielding the sun from his eyes. It was his father; he watched as this figure walked onto the deck to get a better view, and then it happened. The prodigal could not believe it. Still several hundred yards away from home, and he realized it was his father. Then he stepped off the deck onto the dirt road and his stride quickened until he actually saw his father the one he had walked away from break into a run! He hadn't seen his father run for many years; in his later years, walking was the only exercise he had taken. But this day was different; this day was packed with hope, answered prayer, and a new beginnings. His father no longer felt any age restraint or weariness in his body. He actually started running! As the prodigal stood bewildered and amazed in unbelief, his father was now sprinting toward him like a young man running for the finish line. The prodigal son was the finish line; in fact, he was the prize, and he was the trophy his father had been waiting for many months to hold in his arms. This was the day when the father ran!

God is exactly the same, always running toward the prodigal sons and daughters longing to embrace them back, because no matter what has happened on the road of prodigal living, never forget "there is always a way back."

Chapter 13

He Didn't Get What
He Was Expecting

The prodigal had rehearsed all that he would say to his father; he had gone over it so many times on the long journey. If his father would just take him back as one of the servants, he would be satisfied. He was not going to offer any excuses; there weren't any, and defending his actions was not an option. He had no defense! He had left home with his inheritance, nice clothes, and a few of his worldly possessions, and now he returns with no money, torn and dirty clothes, and guilt written all over his face. What could he expect? Maybe a good lecture is a telling off by his father and disgrace in the family by being reduced to servant status. He knew he didn't deserve anything. He wasn't expecting favors of any kind, perhaps a bed, food, and work that was all he could hope for. But he didn't get what he was expecting! He got far more than what he was expecting. He became the recipient of grace!

Think of this scene. the son was amazed as his father came rushing toward him, panting for breath yet with a huge smile all over his face. His father's eyes were gleaming with excitement. He was the embodiment of grace as he ran toward him. No words were necessary; in fact, his father didn't give him time for words—he wrapped his arms around him and wept upon him until his hot tears ran down the prodigal's neck. He was embracing his son so tightly as he showered him with kisses. These were the kisses of compassion and forgiveness and the embrace of grace! For the prodigal to feel the warm embrace of his father and his hot tears of joy rubbing onto his face, it broke the condemnation that had overwhelmed him for many months. He had walked long miles on his journey home expecting to be treated at best as one of the hired servants. Instead of humiliation, he got restoration, and instead of his father's wrath and judgment, he received grace! The two walked back to the little farmhouse. His father's arm wrapped around his son's shoulder, like two long lost friends who never wanted to become estranged again. What the prodigal was expecting is not what he got!

He was now to learn not only is there always a way back, but when anyone dares to walk down the road of repentance and humility, there is "grace" to welcome them home. Let me explain what "the Father's heart" is really like and why the god of the Bible, who gave life and breath to each one of us, is always looking, waiting, and watching for a prodigals' return. It is because His very character is "grace" which in the context of sinners returning back to Him. Grace doesn't look for works. It doesn't demand payment; it doesn't put people on probation. It doesn't appoint them to the status of servants. This is why the gospel of Jesus Christ differs from any other religion—it has absolutely nothing to do with earning favor by seeking to become a better person. Grace is unearned favor, and that is amazing, and that is why John Newton the one-time blasphemous sea trader wrote the song "Amazing Grace."

Grace is amazing! It opens its arms up to the vilest sinner and the most wayward prodigal with the offer of restoration. We live in a world where breaking of the law is punished, be that a traffic violation or in the other extreme murder. Both are offences, the latter of course with a prison sentence. When the sentence is completed, phrases like "he has done his time" or "he has paid his debt to society" are used. A crime becomes punishable by either a fine, community service, probation, or a prison sentence, and in some countries, for murder, there is the death sentence! The one thing the judge, on finding the individual guilty, does not do is offer grace. Many people find it difficult to believe that the gospel of Jesus Christ is the gospel of Grace, where the undeserving sinner (and that is what we all are) can be granted grace (Romans 3:23). The human mind thinks constantly of debt and works to earn favor and that there must be a payment of some kind, in order to merit that favor.

This may sound at first contradictory, but for you and me to obtain God's grace and favor, a payment was necessary. The good news of the gospel is that a payment once and for all has been made. It wasn't a payment of silver or gold; it was a payment far more costly than that. It was the blood of Jesus Christ. I have hopefully made clear that the heart of the Father is one of love and grace, but we must also recognize that His character is holy and just, and because of this, He cannot overlook sin. However, in order to offer us undeserved favor and grace, He has not overlooked sin but rather judged it. He poured out His judgment upon His own Son Jesus Christ, and through the shedding of His blood the price was paid. The Prophet Isaiah described this in his prophecy in Isaiah 53. Please take note of these scriptures (verses 5–6), "But He was wounded for our transgressions, He was bruised for our iniquities the chastisement of our peace was upon Him, and by His stripes we are healed. All we like sheep have gone astray; we have turned everyone to his own way; and the Lord has laid on Him the iniquity of us all." The Message Bible renders it like this, "It was our sins that did that to Him, that ripped and tore and crushed Him—our sins! He took the punishment that made us whole. Through His bruises, we get healed. We're all like sheep what've wondered off and gotten lost. We've all done our thing and gone our own way. And God has piled all our sins, everything we've done wrong on Him."

This is a vivid description of Christ's sacrifice at Calvary where he paid the ultimate price by pouring out his blood and giving his life. The Apostle Peter describes this as follows, "Knowing that you were not redeemed with corruptible things like silver or gold, from your aimless conduct received by tradition of your fathers but with the precious blood of Christ, as of a lamb without blemish and without spot" (1 Peter 1:18–19). Grace is free, but it is not cheap; it was paid for by the blood of Jesus.

In the movie *The Last Emperor*, the child who was anointed as the last emperor of China lives a life of luxury with a thousand eunuchs at his command.

His brother asked him, "What happens when you do wrong?"

He answered, "When I do wrong, someone else is punished."

He demonstrated this by breaking a jar, and one of the servants was beaten. The grace of God is the opposite of that. We have done wrong and sinned, and as a result, the king of the universe (Jesus) was punished! He was wounded for our transgressions and because of this we are offered grace!

To remove this truth from the gospel, we place Christianity on a par with all other man-made religions, but it stands alone and supreme in the truth of the grace of God. The one who called himself the "chief of sinners" and was at one time the architect of the persecution of the new testament church met grace head-on one day on the Damascus road (Acts 9). Saul, as he was then known, was instantly changed by an encounter with Jesus Christ and proclaimed the message of grace from that time on until his death. To a church that Paul had been instrumental in raising up from the spiritual death of idolatrous worship in the city of Ephesus, Paul wrote these words, "But God who is rich in mercy, because of His great love with which He loved us, even when we were dead in trespasses made us alive together with Christ by grace you have been saved" (Ephesians 2:5). He also makes it very clear that the works of human effort could never accomplish this. "For by grace you have been saved through faith and that not of yourselves; it is the gift of God, not of works, lest any should boast" (verse8).

In this chapter, Paul reminds these believers the utter spiritual death and darkness they were once in. He draws a parallel between death and life. There cannot be two more opposites, but Paul is making the case for the grace of God. In verse1, he assures them that they have now been made alive, but they were once dead in trespasses and sins. Isn't this what the father said to the prodigal son, "This my son was dead but is alive again"? The real definition of death is to be separated from life, and Jesus Christ is our life! Paul also infers that they were "lost" in the abyss and sin of this world when he reminds them that their conduct was filled with lust and the selfish desires of their mind (verse 3). But the whole chapter is not to depress them but to assure them that from the depths of sin and a life that was lived without any thought of God, the grace of God had intervened, and more than intervened had brought them into a relationship with God that was totally undeserving, but nevertheless true. From being spiritually dead, they were now alive, and from being lost, they had now been found and were no longer separated from their heavenly Father. This is grace in its simplicity, and this places Christianity and its message along with the cross and resurrection of Jesus Christ into the realm of superiority, which is light years beyond any man-made religion.

The prodigal wasn't expecting grace; in fact, what he was expecting he didn't get! He never expected to hear his father address him as "my son" and to proclaim him alive and found again. Not once on his long journey home had those words ever entered his mind. They were not words that are ordinarily spoken from someone who has been offended. They are not normally the vocabulary of those who have every right to be upset because they have been let down, walked all over as it were, and have given everything with nothing in return. To be led over to the other servants and given a pile of hay to sleep on in the barn with rules read out of when work starts and finishes each day was what he expected and to be left there as his father walked over to the farmhouse, opened the door, and slammed it behind him. That is what he expected, but that is not what he got. Grace doesn't work like that at all. It doesn't bear grudges, it doesn't demote, and it forgives and restores.

Many people, when offended, still quote the Old Testament scripture that says, "An eye for an eye and a tooth for a tooth." If everyone followed the "eye for an eye" principle of justice, observed Gandhi, eventually, the whole world would go blind (Exodus 21:24; Matthew 5:38–42).

The story is told of a Jewish prisoner of war who was in Auschwitz; multitudes were being killed in the gas chambers and before their date with death were starved so that they were like walking skeletons. One such man who survived to tell his story said that one day as he looked through the window of the hut he was held in, a hideous face stared right back at him. The face looked almost demonic; the prisoner turned away but then after a few moments stared again at the window wondering if his mind was playing tricks upon him. The same hideous face stared back, and then he realized it was his own face now emaciated through starvation! That day he fully understood what the consequences of his torture and captivity had done to him. The prodigal had returned with no pretty picture of himself fixed in his mind but rather the opposite. It wasn't that his outward appearance had changed dramatically, but his heart had. It was deep inside himself that he realized what sin had done and the kind of individual he had become since leaving home. He wasn't looking for favors, but grace is unearned favor. This was what was waiting for him.

This was what his father had been waiting to give him, to shower him with forgiveness. Just as the prodigal had rehearsed over and over in his mind what he would do when he left his father's house, his father had rehearsed what he would do when his son returned. To those who feel they have wandered too far away and perhaps have believed the lie that forgiveness is not an offer to them, let me assure you, it is a lie and a lie from the pit of hell. The god who created this world by speaking His word and then created man from the dust of the earth and breathed into him the breath of life is a god who down the ages has proved His love and demonstrated His grace. The Bible hides nothing; it doesn't dress its characters up in their Sunday best and portray them as spotless and holy without faults and blemishes. It hides nothing and refuses to cover up any sin, yet through it all, the forgiveness and grace of God comes through.

There were times of national backsliding and idolatry on Israel's part after so many miracles of God's interventions. What did God do? He rose up prophets to speak the Word of the Lord; the whole purpose was to win them back to a place where they could receive His blessings. Men like Abraham, Moses, David, and Peter to name but a few all had their failings, but God didn't give up on them. He chased them. He ran after them with restoration in mind. He brought Abraham to a place of faith where he and his wife Sarah would dare to believe God for the impossible, a child in their old age.

He appeared to Moses, who had murdered an Egyptian and had been a fugitive in the desert for forty years looking after sheep. He called him to bring deliverance to Israel from the bondage of the slave masters of Egypt. He rescued David from the depths of sinful adultery and restored him in such a manner that the Bible records that David was a man after God's own heart and that he served his generation by the will of God. He rescued Peter from guilt and condemnation after he had denied he ever knew Jesus three times before the crucifixion. He rose from the ashes of denial to the flames of Pentecost to become a great apostle for Jesus Christ. The book of Psalms records times when the psalmist felt depressed and low and is a revelation of the inner heart, along with sins and difficulties that many of us can identify with. But forgiveness is the message of the Bible to a world lost in sin. There is a loving heavenly Father who has provided a way for everyone to find forgiveness. The Apostle Paul wrote these words to the believers in the city of Ephesus and told them they had been "adopted as sons by Jesus Christ to Himself according to the good pleasure of His will, to the praise of the glory of His grace, by which he has made us accepted in the beloved" (Ephesians 1:5–6).

Think for a moment of what Paul is actually teaching here. He uses the word "adoption," but we must never think of believers as being adopted into God's family by some legal procedure as when a court would grant the right to parents to legally adopt a certain child. That is not what the scripture teaches. Paul is referring to something far more dynamic and spiritual, which is called the new birth or the experience of being born again. It is only in this way a person becomes a legal member of God's family or a son or daughter of God. It is this new birth that makes us accepted in the beloved as Paul puts it. The beloved is Jesus Himself. That is how His Father referred to Him at His baptism in the river Jordan, "this is my beloved son in whom I am well pleased." We are accepted into God's family because of what the "beloved Son" Jesus did on our behalf. Paul also teaches in verse 6 that this results "to the praise of the glory of His grace." The grace of God is glorified and praised because it is only by His grace and His unmerited, unearned favor that God could redeem us or make purchase for us by the blood that Jesus poured out for us on the cross (verse 7). Because of Jesus's sacrifice, those who have repented of sin and turned to the Lord have received forgiveness of sins according to the riches of His grace.

Everything God offers us comes from, and by, His grace. Forgiveness and grace are joined together; they are inseparable. There could be no forgiveness unless God was a god of grace; forgiveness flows on the river of grace. Wherever grace is, forgiveness is always available.

The prodigal's father was full of grace; the prodigal had been so far away from him that he had forgotten this. He had forgotten the times when as a boy his father would take him in his arms and show him the love and forgiveness of a father who only ever wanted the best for his son. With everything that had happened during the time, the son had left his father; his recollections of his father's love had been erased. That was and is the problem with so many today. When someone, for whatever reason, decides to distance themselves from God the Father, their heart will grow cold, and human nature has the tendency to forget yesterday's experiences! That kind of scenario played out time and time again throughout the Old Testament when despite miracle after miracle, Israel backslid into idolatry. How could this happen? we might ask, and I'm not referring to just God's provision or victories in battle that the Lord worked on their behalf, as great as they were. But there were many miracles, signs, and wonders that only heaven could perform that left the people in no doubt that God was God. There was supernatural fire over the tabernacle of the Lord by day and a cloud by night, in the wilderness journey that took forty years. Water came from a rock that Moses struck at the command of the Lord, the Red Sea had parted, and all of Egypt's false gods had been exposed by the miracles Moses performed by the hand of God. These are just a few of the amazing miracles, yet Israel—when they had been given their inheritance in the land of Canaan—constantly turned away from the Lord. Such is human nature, and often, the tendency is to become lethargic and forgetful when people choose to live at a distance from the favor and presence of God.

Perhaps you can identify with some of the things I have just written, but no matter how far away from the Father's presence you may feel, He is always ready to run to where you are with the arms of grace, and forgiveness, and welcome you home.

Forgiveness is something that many people struggle with. Some struggle with the receiving of it because, as I have mentioned earlier in the book, they have been led to believe that restoration has to be earned and that God's forgiveness while on offer is no exception. Others struggle with giving forgiveness to the ones who have sinned against them. To illustrate this, Jesus told a story of a king who had a servant who owed him ten thousand talents; after pleading for mercy not to be thrown into prison and for his family's well-being, the king forgave him of all the debt. So the servant left the king's presence debt-free. He hadn't earned this, and he had received this by virtue of the king's kind nature. One would think this man would have left the king overjoyed and thankful for the rest of his life, for the burden of debt that had been lifted from his shoulders. Instead, he meets someone who owed him just a miserly amount compared with what he had owed the king. The poor man pleaded for mercy to the servant, but he would not grant it. Instead, he had him delivered to prison. Can you imagine the utter hypocrisy and hardness of the servant's heart? The story ends with the king finding out what had happened and remonstrating with his servant that after all the mercy and forgiveness he had been shown, he had refused to show the same to someone else. The servant was thrown into prison and experienced torture (Matthew 18:23–35). To apply this story and the moral behind it is quite clear. Every true believer in Jesus Christ who has received grace and forgiveness must recognize the debt they carried which would have cost them eternal life has been removed, and forgiven, by the grace of the King of kings. When others sin against us, whatever it is, it bears no comparison to the debt our king forgave us.

Human nature doesn't see it this way, but the believer has been given a new nature, and it is the principle of this nature to offer forgiveness and to avoid a root of bitterness springing up in one's heart and mind, which brings its own torture!

I remember hearing a true story of a man who came out for prayer at the close of a church service. That evening, the preacher had been speaking on forgiveness, as he went over to the man he noticed his fist clenched tightly. The man asked for prayer because for several years he had not been able to open his fist. When asked what had happened, the man began to tell his story. He had become so angry with another individual that had done something against him that he clenched his fist and raised his arm to strike this man. At that very moment, his fist froze and had been like that ever since that event. The preacher asked him about forgiveness, but the man revealed he had not been able to find it in his heart to forgive. It was not just his fist that had frozen but his heart had too! After a few moments with some encouragement from the preacher, he bowed his head and prayed a prayer of forgiveness. As he did so, the miracle happened, and his hand opened up; the frozen fist was thawed by the love of God and so was his heart!

A prayer of forgiveness in the midst of suffering was uncovered from the horrors of Ravensbruck concentration camp. It was a concentration camp built in 1939 for women. Over ninety thousand women and children perished in Ravensbruck murdered by the Nazis. Corrie Ten Boom who wrote *The Hiding Place* was imprisoned there too. The prayer was found in the clothing of a dead child. This is the prayer:

> O Lord, remember not only the men and woman
> of good will, but also those of ill will. But do not
> remember all of the suffering they have inflicted
> upon us. Instead remember the fruits we have
> borne because of this suffering, our fellowship,
> our loyalty to one another, our humility, our
> courage, our generosity, the greatness of heart
> that has grown from this trouble. When our per-
> secutors come to be judged by you, let all of these
> fruits that we have borne be their forgiveness.

That kind of forgiveness overshadows anything we have suffered at the hands of others that may have caused us to struggle. If you are struggling in this area, don't allow any more time to pass before you release that forgiveness and in so doing release yourself from the root of bitterness. Live free; that is what God has always wanted for every one of us.

I have mentioned some of the struggles people have with forgiveness, either receiving the forgiveness of God or giving forgiveness to others. But there is another struggle in this area that many find difficult, and that is "forgiving ourselves."

A number of years ago, when we were in the UK, we had a visit to our church service one Sunday evening by a coach full of Christians that were touring the area. They had decided to join us for the meeting. The coach driver came into the church with them also and sat through the service. It was as the service was drawing to a close that a number of people came out for prayer for various things, including the coach driver. He had heard that evening of personal stories of people who had come to know the Lord and whose lives had been radically changed. He wept as he stood with head bowed waiting for prayer. When I asked him what he would like me to pray for, he told me the following story.

He had served in the British army during the Falklands War. The British troops had gone over to push back the Argentinean forces that had moved into the Falklands to claim the island as their own. It was one day when our friend the coach driver was involved in one of the battles that he found himself face-to-face with a young Argentinean soldier. He knew he had to act fast as they stood literally face-to-face, and he thrust his bayonet in the stomach of the young soldier, who was no more than about fifteen years of age. The coach driver told us that the young soldier fell to the ground and he died calling out for his mamma. "I have not been able to get that scene from my mind and those words as he called out for his mamma. Do you think God can forgive me?" It was my great joy to lead this man to the Lord Jesus and for him to receive the grace and forgiveness of God. It is one thing to receive forgiveness, but to forgive ourselves can be more difficult for some. However, we must turn again to the Bible the Word of God and learn to live with the truth that whatever we have done He has forgiven us, and if the judge of all the earth declares us forgiven, we must forgive ourselves. Paul had to do that, after all he had done before conversion, including being at the stoning of the first Christian martyr, Stephen, and having others tortured that followed Jesus.

The prodigal didn't get what he expected; grace and forgiveness had wrapped its arms around him, but how could he forgive himself? How could he face other people that knew him and what he had done? He was overcome by the amazing love his father had shown to him; nevertheless, it was difficult as he moved closer to the farmhouse. All kinds of emotions flooded his mind; memories of the security of home and the daily routines that had been such a big part of his life, the hot meals that were served up after a day's work and the happy conversations they had enjoyed around the meal table, friends that would visit and would always be made welcome. His home had been so wonderful; he could hardly come to terms with the fact that he had been foolish enough to have done what he had done.

He took a deep breath as his father strode toward the door and held it open once again for him to enter. As he walked into the living room, it was as though nothing had changed; everything was where it always had been. In one corner was the old armchair in exactly the same place where his father always sat after dinner. The pictures on the walls all told their own story which had indelibly left their mark on his mind. He took a deep breath and just stood taking it all in, but there was just something different as his eyes glanced at the old farmhouse table in the center of the room. It was set with the best plates and cutlery, drinking glasses, and napkins. It only took a moment for him to realize that it was set for a party. His father had prepared for the day when his son would return home.

Billy Graham's daughter Ruth relates her own story of her first marriage breakup and how she eventually when living away from home met a handsome widower. Her children cautioned her to take things slowly as did her siblings. Her dad Billy Graham suggested that she bring him to meet them before rushing into another marriage. She says she was headstrong and strong willed and rather than do what they had suggested, she got married on New Year's Eve. She knew after the first day she had made a terrible mistake, and after about a week, she decided to run away from the marriage. Sometime later when her family heard the news, she decided she would return home to see her parents. She felt ashamed and guilty, and even worse than that, she felt she had brought shame to the family and with her dad being Billy Graham that only seemed to add to the guilt. She drove to the family home and pulled up in the driveway not knowing what to expect. As she got out of her car and closed the door, she looked across to the family home, and there was her dad Billy Graham with his arms wide open to welcome her back. Ruth says that day her dad showed her by his actions welcome and forgiveness, the very heart of her heavenly Father.

Please remember, "there is always a way back."

Chapter 14

It's Party Time

The prodigal couldn't believe his ears. Was he dreaming or was this reality? *I deserve nothing*, he thought, and *I'm being welcomed home, not just welcomed home, but there is a party about to be thrown in my honor!* "But the Father said to his servants, Bring out the best robe and put it on him and put a ring on his hand and sandals on his feet. And bring the fatted calf here and kill it, and let us eat and be merry; for this my son was dead and is alive again; he was lost and is found. And they began to be merry" (Luke 15:22–24). In the Message Bible, it renders what the father said in words like this, "Bring a clean set of clothes and dress him, put the family ring on his finger and sandals on his feet. Then get a grain-fed heifer and roast it. We're going to have a feast. We're going to have a wonderful time! My son is here given up for dead and now alive! Given up for lost and now found."

Jesus includes this vivid description of the prodigal's homecoming to drive home the truth that when any prodigal returns to his Father, heaven throws a party. God is not against parties and celebrating good times, in fact in Luke 15, He told two other stories that illustrate this same truth (verse 4–7), "Suppose one of you had a hundred sheep and lost one. Wouldn't you leave the ninety-nine in the wilderness and go after the lost one until you found it? When found you can be sure you would put it across your shoulders, rejoicing, and when you got home call your friends and neighbors saying,

'Celebrate with me! I've found my lost sheep!' Count on it—there's more joy in heaven over one sinner's rescued life than over ninety-nine good people in no need of rescue."

There is also the story of the lost coin (verses 8–10). Imagine a woman who has ten coins and loses one. Won't she light a lamp and scour the house, looking in every nook and cranny until she finds it? And when she finds it, you can be sure she will call her friends and neighbors: "Celebrate with me! I found my lost coin! Count on it—that's the kind of party God's angels throw every time one lost soul turns to God."

Let's just consider these stories or parables for a moment. As I wrote in the introduction to this book, the context in which Jesus told these stories was that the religious leaders the Pharisees had accused Him, not so much of teaching and talking to sinners but eating with them. The Jewish culture was that of a shame and honor system. The motivation behind much of what took place was to seek honor for oneself and avoid shame. The fact that the good shepherd would leave the ninety-nine sheep behind to seek the one which was lost was to portray the love, compassion, and forgiveness of God. But what about the ninety-nine sheep he left on the mountain side? Was there some sarcasm in the reference to the ninety-nine righteous persons who needed no repentance? After all, the apostle taught that we have all sinned, and therefore, all need to come to repentance (Romans 3:23). The same Pharisees who had looked down on Him for eating with the tax collectors and sinners were known for being self-righteous and in no need of repentance.

What good shepherd would leave ninety-nine sheep unattended to search for one? Remember the Prophet Isaiah refers to human beings as being like sheep, when he says, "All we like sheep have gone astray; we have turned everyone to our way . . ." (Isaiah 53:6). Sheep are noted for their wandering away! I think the whole parable was stressing the point and truth that the good shepherd, God the Father, will do whatever it takes to rescue those who are lost. They are the ones who admit and know they have gone astray. Many will never admit that truth; the Pharisees were among that group, and that is why on another occasion when Jesus was speaking to the chief priests and elders, Jesus said the publicans and sinners will enter the kingdom of God before you. When He finds the one who is lost, He will carry it back on His shoulders to safety and to great rejoicing even a party!

The story of the lost coin has the same theme. The ten silver coins refer to a piece of jewelry with ten coins on it which was worn by brides, similar to how brides today would wear a wedding ring. To lose a wedding ring is not something that any bride would want to do, but if that happened, she would turn the house upside down (so to speak) to find that ring. She too would invite friends around to her house to celebrate when she found the coin (ring). It's all about the lost being found and heaven throwing a party when they come back home.

The father had waited patiently and believed that one day his son would return, and for that return, he had prepared. Make no mistake, our heavenly Father is not just waiting for prodigals; He is searching for them and has prepared very well for a party and celebration on their return!

Before the first sin that caused the whole human race to fall and drift away from the creator, God had a plan. It was a plan that was conceived in eternity, prophesied down the ages, and came to fruition one day in a little town called Bethlehem. It was there a child was born, but this was no ordinary child. This was God the Father's gift to a lost world; it was the gift of His Son Jesus Christ. He was a gift, a savior that not only did angels announced His arrival in this world, but all the host of heaven must have gazed down in awe at what God had done. The eternal Son was now clothed in human flesh and had stepped into a world that was under the power of the prince of darkness, Satan himself. He who announced Himself as the "light of the world" had now come to expose the darkness. The God of eternity and the ages had now come to bring the kingdom of God into what had become a kingdom of darkness. Of course there was conflict; this was to be the conflict of the ages, but the battle was not won with the usual weapons of war. To the casual observer, it would appear that the Son of God and the plan of God were crushed at Calvary. It was there that a cross was erected, and on that cross, the

Son of God was crucified. But the plan didn't end at Calvary; death wasn't His end but rather where His work was completed. The cry that came out from the swollen lips of the Savior as He hung on that cross with every bone in His body out of joint must have rocked the very foundations of hell. The cry wasn't "I am finished," but "it is finished." The divine plan for a perfect sacrifice for sin was fulfilled, and the resurrection three days later would testify to the truth of who He is and what He had done.

This was all part of the preparation to provide a way home for everyone who would be prepared to make the journey. And it was vitally necessary, for it was on this basis that the Father could prepare a celebration party.

Immediately, the prodigal stepped over the threshold of the home that His Father had been waiting to welcome him back to; he heard these words, "Bring out the best robe and put it on him." Nothing was spared, the best robe had to be brought out, and the servants knew exactly where it was and which one it was. This was not a second hand robe that someone else had worn, this was reserved, and it had been purchased and kept under wraps for this special day. For a celebration of life, it was only fitting the best robe should be worn. This was not a day to be frugal, but a day that called for the very best to be lavished upon his son.

The best robe anyone can wear is not any earthly garment made from the finest and best fabrics, but rather a robe that no human eye can see it's a robe of righteousness that only God the Father can give to those who genuinely turn to Him in repentance and faith.

It wasn't fitting for the prodigal to sit down at the banqueting table and enjoy the party in clothes that still smelled of the pigsty. His Father wanted to see him in different clothes, wearing the best robe, as one who was the center of attention at the party.

The Prophet Isaiah spoke of a robe of righteousness saying, "I will greatly rejoice in the Lord, my soul shall be joyful in my God; for He has clothed me with the garments of salvation" (Isaiah 61:10). Jesus also told a story regarding wedding garments (Matthew 22:11). Everyone invited to this wedding was given particular robes to wear, but the story continues that one man managed to find a way through to the celebration without a wedding garment; he was quickly removed! To be in the king's presence demands the right attire!

It was God who made the first garment in the garden of Eden for Adam and Eve to wear when their nakedness was uncovered by the loss of the presence and glory of God. Animal skins provided the first covering garments. We must understand that to come into the King of king's presence, this is the most awesome privilege we could ever be granted, and yet today, millions still believe that it is their good works and so-called decent lives that bring them acceptance. Again, Isaiah the prophet makes it abundantly clear that this cannot be the case when he says, "But we are all like an unclean thing, and all our righteousnesses are like filthy rags . . ." (Isaiah 64:6).

The prodigal stood in the old farmhouse in his own filthy rags, not just stained with pig dirt but with reckless and extravagant sin. But His Father took the robe from the servant and, with a huge smile on his face, placed the robe around his son. Instantly, the prodigal's whole appearance was transformed, and tears of joy rolled down his cheeks, his lips trembled as he tried to hold back his emotions, but failed to do so.

Paul the apostle wrote, "For He made Him (Jesus) to be sin for us that we might become the righteousness of God in Him" (2 Corinthians 5:21). Jesus took our sin that we can be clothed with His righteousness. That's a wonderful exchange!

The truth of this is also confirmed in Romans 4, Paul writing about Abraham that he believed God regarding the promise made to him that he would become the father of many nations (verse 17), and because of Abraham's faith, it was accounted to him for righteousness (verse 22). Paul then goes on to say that this was not written for Abraham's sake alone but for all who would believe; to these God would impute His righteousness upon them, on the basis of Jesus's death and resurrection (verses 24–25). What this really means is that God covers with His righteousness all those who truly believe; He places His robe, the best robe we could ever wear upon us. From that moment, God looks upon as righteous, He sees what no one else can see with the natural eye. He sees Christ's righteousness covering our filthy rags.

The Prophet Isaiah writes of the "garment of praise" that God gives in place of a spirit of heaviness (Isaiah 61:3). The spirit of heaviness must have been the prodigal's constant companion when he worked in the pigsty and on the long trek home. But that kind of spirit is not at home in a party. This was party time; this was celebration time. The atmosphere of heaven is filled with praise; the scenes we see from the writings of the Apostle John in the book of Revelation are of multitudes worshipping and praising God. Men and women are so thankful for the miracle of salvation that heaven erupts with vibrant praise (Revelation 5).

No one could convince the prodigal as his father wrapped the best robe around him that this was a dream or figment of his imagination. He was there; he was the recipient of amazing grace, love, and forgiveness. He was accepted again! When anyone comes back to the Lord and really encounters His love and grace praise and worship will automatically flow from a heart touched by heaven. Praise and worship become a lifestyle, not a few minutes of exercise during a Christian service while the worship group is singing. Too many attend church worship services and become onlookers and spectators instead of becoming participators. They never seem to "enter His gates" as the psalmist puts it with praise which makes me wonder sometimes what kind of experience if any have these people really had. When Jesus was telling the story of the prodigal son, He was revealing the kind of character, grace, and love that His Father has. Our delight should be to enter into His presence and to enter into His gates (throne room) with praise. This story is all about a very real loving heavenly Father who longs for us to enjoy His presence. Remember this was the mistake the prodigal made in the first place; he wanted to be as far away as possible from his father's presence! I don't think for one moment he would make the same mistake again. I encourage every reader of this book to make praise a priority, learn to love the Father's presence, and learn to receive His blessings of grace.

The robe was not the only thing the prodigal received that day. His father placed upon his son's finger "the family ring." The prodigal had walked away from family, and in his darkest moments and sleepless nights, he couldn't imagine ever being accepted again. But no sooner had the Father placed the best robe upon him; he also placed the ring on his finger. As the prodigal looked at this ring, his shoulders shook, and he couldn't hold back the sobs. This ring said it all; his father didn't need to make any more speeches or announcements the ring made them for him. The family ring signified he was back, he was accepted, and he was home! This ring would remind him of his restored relationship and favor that was now once again his.

The Apostle John wrote, "Behold what manner of love the Father has bestowed upon us that we should be called the children of God! Therefore the world does not know us, because it did not know Him. Beloved now we are the children of God; and it has not yet been revealed what we shall be, but we know that when He is revealed we shall be like Him, for we shall see Him as He is. And everyone who has this hope in him purifies himself just as He is pure (1 John 3:1–3).

The psalmist writes, "God sets the solitary in families, He brings out those who are bound into prosperity; but the rebellious dwell in a dry land" (Psalm 68:6).

The prodigal was now back with his family. He knew the reality too well of being bound in the vices of this world and had literally dwelt in a dry land, a land scourged by famine. But that was the past that was confined now to his yesterdays; his present situation was that he was now welcomed back into the family home, dressed in the best robe, and had the family ring on his finger. He couldn't have wished for anything better than this. He almost had to pinch himself to see if this was all real.

This is the amazing plan and purpose of God that Paul writes about to the believers in the city of Ephesus. I remind you that they had a history of idolatry that really was founded in occult practices; the city was full of magical arts and idolatrous replicas and trinkets that were associated with the huge statue of Diana. But Paul wrote these words to these converts to Christ, "Now therefore you are no longer strangers and foreigners but fellow citizens with the saints (believers) and members of the household of God" (Ephesians 2:19). They were no longer wondering exiles removed from the life and presence of God. They had come home; they were family members of the kingdom of God!

For the prodigal, it really couldn't get any better, and then he was presented with a new pair of sandals. The old ones were well worn and had walked into the vice dens of the city and eventually the pigsty. His father was presenting him with new sandals which represented a new walk. Everything of the old was quickly fading into the past, and the new was filled with great promise and hope.

Jeremiah, the prophet, gave a great promise to God's people. It is recorded in Jeremiah 29:11 ". . . For I know the thoughts that I think toward you, says the Lord, thoughts of peace and not of evil to give you a hope and a future."

This verse captures the sentiments of our heavenly Father's love and desire for each one of us irrespective of our past, as long as we are willing to make the journey home. The prodigal had walked that road and made the journey; it was now "party time." Parties are times for celebration, food, and music, and to provide the food the fatted calf was brought out, there was nothing spared for this party! This was a day of celebration like no other; to a young man who didn't deserve anything, he was being lavished with love and gifts, from a father who had waited so long for this day.

Tony Campolo shares a true story about "a party for a prostitute" in "The Kingdom of God Is a Party." Tony had traveled from the East Coast of the USA to Hawaii. America is a big country, and there are time differences in many states. Traveling to Hawaii, he relates that three o'clock in the morning feels like nine. Finding it difficult to sleep, he wandered around the streets of Honolulu at three-thirty in the morning looking for somewhere to eat. He found a little place eventually and ordered a cup of coffee and a donut. It wasn't particularly the kind of place he would have chosen by any stretch of the imagination, but in the middle of the night, there wasn't much choice. As he sat there drinking his coffee and eating his donut, the door opened and in walked eight or nine prostitutes. They were quite loud and crude in their conversations which he couldn't help but overhear. He was just about to leave when he overheard one of the woman sitting near him tell the others that it was her birthday the following day and said she was going to be thirty-nine years old.

One of the women sarcastically commented, "What, do you want me to do get you a cake and throw a birthday party for you?"

"I've never had a birthday party in my whole life. Why should I have one now?" replied the woman sitting near to Tony.

When the women had left, Tony asked the guy who had served him with his coffee and donut if these women came in every night at the same time. He told Tony that the woman who had sat next to him was called Agnes, and she did come in every night. By this time, he was growing very inquisitive and asked Tony why he wanted that information. Tony told him about his idea of throwing a birthday party for Agnes the following night. The guy called his wife out from the kitchen and told her of Tony's idea. They all agreed it was a great idea. Harry, the guy who had served Tony, insisted that he would make the birthday cake, and Tony told them he would be in early the next night and decorate the place. Tony was back at two-thirty the next morning and had made a cardboard sign which read "Happy Birthday Agnes." Everything was looking good with all the decorations, and it seemed that the news of a party had reached about every prostitute in Honolulu, and the place was packed. At exactly three-thirty that morning, the door swung open and in walked Agnes with her friends.

Everyone was ready for their coming, and as they walked in, they shouted "happy birthday!" Agnes looked like she was going to faint; she was stunned as they all sang "happy birthday, dear Agnes." Then Harry came out with cake and candles. Agnes broke into sobs and tears and couldn't blow the candles out, so Harry did it for her. Harry then insisted she cut the cake, but Agnes was so overcome and asked if she could take the cake down the road to her mother's house to show her as she had never had a birthday cake.

Everyone stood in silence as Agnes left. Tony broke the silence by asking if he could pray. He prayed for Agnes for her salvation and that she would know the blessing of God. When Tony had finished praying, Harry said to him, "You never told me you were a preacher. What kind of church do you belong to?"

Tony's reply was just brilliant, "I belong to a church that throws birthday parties for prostitutes at three-thirty in the morning."

Harry said, "No, you don't. There's no church like that. If there was, I'd join it. I'd join a church like that!"

If only people would realize that this is the kind of church that Jesus wants. The old hymn that is called "Just As I Am, Without One Plea" portrays this truth that anyone can make the journey back to the Father "just as they are," in the rags of sin and shame, and He is waiting, waiting to welcome, forgive, and transform.

Jesus was teaching the tremendous truth that His heavenly Father loves to do the same. He likes throwing parties. He along with the angels rejoices every time a sinner turns in repentance and faith to Him (Luke 15:10). And when that happens, out come the gifts He has already prepared. He is only too pleased to shower upon His sons and daughters that were once lost and spiritually dead. The book of Revelation (19:6–7) describes a great banquet and party that will take place one day. Great multitudes with a voice that will sound like many waters and mighty thunder will declare, "Alleluia! For the Lord God Omnipotent reigns! Let us be glad and rejoice and give Him glory, for the marriage of the Lamb has come, and His wife has made herself ready!" It will be a party to surpass all parties, and words cannot express what surprises He has in store.

As the prodigal sat at the table in his father's house, to be home was all he had longed for, but the father had prepared surprise gifts to lavish upon him. The apostle Paul wrote, "Eye has not seen, nor ear heard, nor have entered into the heart of man the things that God has prepared for those who love Him. But God is revealing them to us through His Spirit. For the Spirit searches all things, yes the deep things of God" (2 Corinthians 1:9–10).

It's only family members that get to share in these things, those who love being in the Father's presence!

I think at the very moment the prodigal realized that His father had prepared a party, he must have felt like the Shulamite woman who said referring to the one she loved (the Lord, "He brought me into His banqueting house and His banner over me was love" (Song of Solomon 2:4).

Did you catch this amazing truth, and have I dispelled all the wrong thoughts that may have lurked in your mind that you can never be accepted again? God is in the restoration business; the party is prepared, and God is waiting for you to make the journey home, and He'll come running. The balloons are ready, the cake has been made in your honor, and heaven is waiting to sing "Welcome Home." Remember, "there is always a way back."

Chapter 15

What He Thought He Would Become He Didn't

The only thought in the prodigal's mind was that his father may accept him back, but he couldn't hope for anything more than becoming a hired servant. Anything would be better than living in the mess he had gotten himself into. But when the Lord saves any repentant sinner or restores a returning prodigal, it is not to a status of a servant but to sonship. There is a vast difference between the two. Let's just consider this for a moment.

Servants

Servants are people who perform duties for another person. The word often was rendered slave in the Bible. A servant does the bidding of his master or employer. A servant was a personal attendant. Joseph in the Old Testament was sold into slavery by his brothers and became a slave or servant in the house of his master Potiphar.

Sons

Sons are different from servants. Sons have all the rights of family membership, and they are people who have bestowed upon them the privileges of being a family member. It's the difference between someone working in a huge family business and carrying out assigned duties which are equivalent to a "servant" or employee and someone who is a son of the owner of the business, who inherits by virtue of his family membership the benefits of the business.

Many believe that salvation and favor with God is earned by works, as stated earlier in the book. These people have no understanding of what the grace of God really is. There are also many who have come to know the Lord and yet still fail to see the truth and privileges of sonship. Their lives are full of good works which is very commendable, but they don't balance everything with the privileges of sonship. Any father would be well pleased with a son or daughter, who willingly wanted to be a blessing to them with acts of service and gratitude, for the privileges bestowed upon them. But there are also and must be times when sons and daughters just sit and enjoy family privileges.

The Apostle Paul was careful to balance these two truths together of sonship and servanthood. Consider some of the following passages:

"Blessed be the God and Father of our Lord Jesus Christ, who has blessed us with every spiritual blessing in the heavenly places in Christ, just as He chose us in Him before the foundation of the world, that we should be holy and without blame before Him in love, having predestined us to adoption as sons by Jesus Christ to Himself, according to the good pleasure of His will, to the praise of the glory of His grace, by which he made us accepted in the Beloved" (Ephesians 1:3–6).

In these verses, Paul brings out the truth of sonship and uses the word "adoption." I stress again this is not just a legal adoption as we would understand in modern days but rather an adoption that takes place through the work of the Holy Spirit when a person is "born again."

Peter uses the word *begotten* to describe this new birth. The word when used especially of a male parent means "to procreate or generate (offspring)."

In Matthew chapter 1, the chapter commences with the words "the book of the genealogy of Jesus Christ," and then proceeds in the verses that follow up to verse sixteen, of who begat who, e.g., "Abraham begat Isaac, Isaac begat Jacob," etc. In other words, Abraham was the father of Isaac, and Isaac was the father of Jacob and so on. It is interesting to note that when we read of Jesus Christ (verse 18), it says that Mary the mother of Jesus was found to be with child of the Holy Spirit. Joseph was not his father; he was his guardian. Jesus always referred to God as his Father.

In 1 Chronicles, there are numerous chapters given to genealogy which a lot of people like to skip over when reading the Bible, but we have verse after verse telling us who begat who. If the word "begat" means as already stated "to procreate or generate," then Peter is clearly teaching that the person who repents and believes the gospel is actually "begotten of God."

"Blessed be the God and Father of our Lord Jesus Christ, who according to His abundant mercy has begotten us again to a living hope through the resurrection of Jesus Christ from the dead" (1 Peter 1:3).

Just as the birth of Jesus Christ was by a supernatural conception of the Holy Spirit, in a similar way, the believer is "born again" by a supernatural act of the Holy Spirit and becomes a recipient of the life of God (1 John 5:12).

With this spiritual new birth comes "every spiritual blessing in Christ." Sons and daughters of God must appreciate and learn to partake of these blessings. They are reserved for those who are family members and not just simply slaves!

In the following passage, as Paul writes to the Philippians, he addresses himself as a "bond servant."

"Paul and Timothy bondservants of Jesus Christ..." (Philippians 1:1)

Peter also called himself a "bond servant."

"Simon Peter, a bondservant and apostle of Jesus Christ . . ." (2 Peter 1:1)

Probably the best definition of the word "bond servant" is someone who is devoted to another to the disregard of one's own interests. It is when we appreciate the privileges of sonship we willingly make ourselves "bond servants." Both Paul and Peter had much to thank

God for as they witnessed the grace of God in their lives. Paul was the great persecutor of the church who was basically a terrorist, with an intent on putting a stop to the Christian gospel message. And Peter, the one who promised so much, but when the real test came before the crucifixion, as to whether he knew Jesus and was one of His followers, he denied this three times. No wonder having received God's grace, despite what they had done, these two men were only too willing to make themselves "bond servants" of Jesus Christ.

But what greater example can we call on to illustrate the truth of being both sons and bond servants than that of Jesus Christ Himself! The scripture that springs to mind before any others is found in Philippians 2:5–8.

"Let this mind be in you which was also in Christ Jesus, who being in the form of God did not consider it robbery to be equal with God, but made Himself of no reputation, taking the form of a bondservant, and coming in the likeness of men. And being found in appearance as a man, He humbled Himself and became obedient to the point of death even the death on the cross."

The Message says, "when the time came He set aside the privileges of deity and took on the status of a slave."

The Son of God was with the Father when in the beginning, it was He who framed the worlds by the Word of God. It was the Son who, when He was being baptized by John, saw the heavens open and heard these wonderful words from His Father, "This is My beloved Son in whom I am well pleased." And yet it was the beloved Son who, as Son and servant, sought always to be in the will of the Father. It was at the garden of Gethsemane—just prior to His betrayal, arrest, and crucifixion—that He prayed the kind of prayer that only a servant could pray, "If it be possible let this cup pass from Me, nevertheless not My will but Your will be done." This prayer came from the depths of His being as He looked, as it were, into a cup of suffering and crucifixion. This was nearing the climax of His earthly ministry, in which He had always sought to be in the Father's will, to do what the Father told Him to do, and to speak the truth that His Father gave to Him to share with a lost world.

After the healing of the impotent man at the pool of Bethesda, Jesus declared, "the Son can do nothing of Himself, but what He sees the Father do, for whatever He does the Son also does in like manner" (John 5:19).

The last words as He died upon the cross where "it is finished" and "into your hands I commit My spirit." To His very last breath Jesus did the will of His Father and finished the work as a servant Son that had been assigned to Him by the Father.

After the crucifixion and resurrection, the disciples must have thought much about these things and especially to the time when they were debating who would be the greatest among them. They would remember the time when Jesus took a basin and a towel and washed their feet and told them this was done as an example that they should follow (John 13:15). He also told them that a servant is not greater than his master, nor is he who is sent greater than he who sent him (John 13:16). These things must have been impressed indelibly upon their minds as they remembered these important life lessons.

They were to go on to blaze the good news of the gospel across the then known world but would never forget who they were, sons with all the privileges of being in God's family. And as servants who were so thankful for the grace of God, they were only too willing to be also bond servants of Jesus Christ.

The prodigal thought he would be assigned servant duties; that's what he thought he would be given when he returned, but what he thought he would become, he didn't! The Father had other plans, as He does for everyone who is willing to make the journey home. Don't allow the devil to deceive you. The plan of God is to restore and shower upon you the blessings of sonship, and true sons and daughters find their hearts so overwhelmed with God's goodness, love, and grace that they are only too pleased to become bond servants.

The UK songwriter and worship leader Graham Kendrick wrote a song entitled "The Servant King" which is part of the album *Ultimate Worship.*

The lyrics of this song express the servanthood of Jesus and our call to follow Him and His example.

> From heaven you came helpless babe
> Entered our world, your glory veiled
> Not to be served but to serve
> And give Your life that we might live

This servant king who came back from the dead by way of resurrection has provided a way back for all prodigals not to a life as mere servants but as sons who willingly will want to serve. As the prodigal stood in awe of the lavish welcome and love shown to him by his father he must have surely made an inner vow and resolution. A resolution that he would never make the same mistake again, and that he would willingly serve the one who had showered him with so much love and grace. Wherever you are and whatever your personal story is, to serve the one who is willing to restore you to far more than you could ever hope to be, will not be a chore but a delight. Remember, "there is always a way back."

Chapter 16

Adjustments to Restoration

Music, dancing, and a feast in honor of the prodigal's return could be heard way beyond the walls of the little farmhouse (Luke 15:25). Although the prodigal sat there in utter amazement at the party atmosphere and the welcome home he had received, it would be in the days that lay ahead he would have to come to terms with some adjustments that would have to be made. It wasn't so much adjustment back into the family life that he had walked away from, but adjustments that had to be made in his mind. The guilt and shame that had walked with him on the long journey home were something he would have to deal with along with the torment of his mind and memories, although he was forgiven, embraced, and restored by his father. It would be great to simply write of restoration and give the impression that ever after of everything was wonderful, and the prodigal slipped right back into normal family life. The story doesn't really tell us much about that, apart from the fact that his brother wasn't too happy about the welcome home party; but I will refer to his attitude later. The truth is that the enemy of our souls, whose desire is to do all he can to draw away prodigals from home and into reckless and extravagant sinning, is not content to give prodigals an easy ride. The battle the prodigal would face would be a battle of his thoughts and mind, and also with self-condemnation, as mentioned earlier in the book.

Forgiving ourselves is often more difficult to accept than God's forgiveness. There would also be the thoughts of what others were thinking about him. He knew his father had showered him with love, but would his old friends, whom he had walked away from, accept him again?

Guilt is not a bad thing; it is actually healthy when it turns us away from sin, but when it continues to plague us every day of our lives, it becomes condemnation. It is condemnation that will drag people down into depression, and depression is a downward spiral that cuts people off from joy, happiness, and any dreams they may have had for the future. This is one of the enemy's major strategies that he seeks to use upon every returning prodigal, in an attempt to stop them from enjoying what God has provided. The enemy hates the thought of restoration and will bombard the human mind with self-condemnation. This of course is the opposite to the heart of the message of the gospel. The Apostle Paul declared, "There is no condemnation to those who are in Christ who walk not according to the flesh (or selfish desires) but according to the Spirit" (Romans 8:1).

When the prodigal returned and his father threw a party and showered him with gifts, this was all intended to show his son that he was welcomed back into the family with all its benefits and blessings. There was no thought in his father's mind that his son would live with depression, low self-esteem, guilt, and condemnation, for the rest of his life. For the prodigal to sink into that way of life would have been so disappointing to his father. His father would have looked on in anguish, watching his son day by day struggle with those issues, rather than enjoy the blessings of being back in the family home.

It was guilt and shame along with need that brought the prodigal back. God the Father had so worked upon the prodigal's heart and life to bring him to the point where he turned his steps and his heart toward home. As already mentioned, it was quite a journey; it was a humbling process. But the plan was always restoration and blessing when he returned.

For every prodigal in this modern age, let me make it clear that the will of God is complete restoration so they may live the rest of their lives enjoying the benefits of a relationship with the Father.

For that experience to take place, several things need to happen. There must be an absolute conviction that restoration means restoration to everything that was lost. Settling for half measures such as a welcome home and then servanthood is not the divine agenda; it is sonship that is the Father's plan and purpose. Once that purpose is embraced by faith, every other negative thought must be rigorously rejected that would seek to bring condemnation and constant reminders of the old life. Of course, what happened when the prodigal was in a far country? He would never erase from his mind, but he would have the choice as to whether those thoughts remained paramount in his thinking. They have to be replaced with the Word of God and truth. Jesus declared, "You will know the truth and the truth will make you free" (John 8:32). It is the truth that we know and embrace that sets us free. And for that to take place, it has to enter our spirit not simply be written in the Bible.

The Apostle Paul wrote to the Corinthian church about the pulling down of strongholds (2 Corinthians 10:4–6), "For the weapons of our warfare are not carnal but mighty in God for pulling down strongholds, casting down arguments and every high thing that exalts itself against the knowledge of God bringing every thought into captivity to the obedience of Christ, and being ready to punish all disobedience when your obedience is fulfilled."

There is always a battle from the enemy of our souls over every word the Lord has spoken, and there will undoubtedly be a battle over "there is now no condemnation to those who are in Christ . . ." Please remember who penned those words in Romans 8:1 by the inspiration of the Holy Spirit. It was Paul, the one-time terror of the church, whose resumé wasn't deserving of any favors from God. But then neither is ours; it is by grace and by grace alone that we can find any favor with God. It is this truth that we must stand upon and contend with against all the attacks of condemnation the devil will bring. Remember the prodigal returned in humility, and humility is what the Lord always requires. But I stress the point that we must not mistake humility for "false humility" which lures people into the trap of thinking themselves to be unworthy failures whose only hope is to just make it back to the Father's house, and in that to be content! Believe me, they are never content, and neither is anyone who allows those thought patterns to control their mind. This is a daily battle that will only be won by bringing the Word of God which is the truth to combat every idle negative thought. These strongholds of the mind must be pulled down, and the mind must be renewed for transformation to take place (Romans 12:1–3).

Yesterday's failures must not be allowed to ruin the destiny that God has planned for the rest of one's life. Our history is not our destiny! We can learn from past mistakes and sins, and we can be thankful for the grace of God, but we must accept and live in the Father's plan and purpose for welcoming every prodigal home.

Adjustments are inevitable. The prodigal had been away for some time, and he would have to face people again, face those from whom he walked away. There are no shortcuts to these things. It's like returning to the church one walked away from. The spiritual people will be only too pleased to see prodigals return; they will regard such as answers to prayer. There may be others who will not react in that way—these are people who have forgotten the truth that they have been forgiven and do not live in the daily revelation of the grace of God. There are also other adjustments to be made if we have offended people or let them down; these are the adjustments of reconciliation that call for apologies. The truly repentant prodigal will not shy from these but will recognize the grace shown to him by the Father and will want to pursue peace with all men. Too often people will try and shortcut these things, but there are no shortcuts if we genuinely want reconciliation. Heaven did not shortcut anything when it came to the sacrifice the Son of God was to make for the sins of the whole world. The god of heaven looked down upon the ultimate evil the world could do to His Son. He listened to the cry that came from the lips of His Son as He prayed in the garden of Gethsemane, "If it is possible let this cup pass from me nevertheless not my will but your will be done." The God who had created the universe by speaking, and had created legions of angels, could have uttered just one word, and heaven's angel armies would have swooped down from the eternal regions and annihilated every living soul that sought to do Jesus harm. But there was to be no shortcuts! The Son had to become the ultimate sacrifice for sin and take upon Himself the full weight of the judgment of a holy God.

Apologies are only difficult to the one who still harbors pride. And reconciliation and forgiveness is only difficult to the offended if they have forgotten the amazing grace of God they have received from the Father of love. Little children who throw a tantrum when told to say sorry often find this difficult. After a few words from their parents, they may mumble something which is very difficult to decipher in an attempt to just get through the exercise. But loving parents will always insist that they speak clearly and that they are sorry for their bad behavior. To shortcut this would be to do the child a disservice and sow wrong seeds which in future will germinate into the child believing that bad behavior can just be dismissed without consequences.

When humility reigns, we are prepared to take whatever action needs to be undertaken to put matters right, whether that is for restoration or for restitution. No shortcuts should be sought! The Bible teaches that God's peace and His joy can only be experienced when we seek to live at peace with others. As we practice forgiveness and whenever necessary ask for forgiveness to those we may have offended, the peace of God will again flood our lives. To do these things is to live in a way where we are submitted to God and His word. The book of James teaches that "God resists the proud and gives grace to the humble and that we are to submit to God, and to resist the devil and he will flee from you" (James 4:6–7).

In order to live above condemnation and to not allow our past to destroy our present and future, these adjustments are necessary; they may not always be easy, but they are worth it. To live in the peace of God is something that money can never buy, and this same peace will keep our hearts and minds from being robbed of what is rightfully ours by the grace of God. This is the lifestyle any truly repentant prodigal will pursue when they have embraced the truth that "there is always a way back."

Chapter 17

The Other Prodigal Son

We come to a very interesting part of the story as Jesus draws it to a close. We find there is another prodigal son! This son hadn't left home and led the kind of life his younger brother had, but he was a "prodigal" just the same (Luke 15:28). We need to think about what Jesus was actually teaching and why He included the elder brother in this story. So let's look at what exactly had been happening. I remind you that the younger son had asked for his inheritance, which was really tantamount to saying he wished his father dead. The focus at the close of this story then turns to the elder brother who to put it mildly was not too pleased with the fact that his father had thrown a party for his brother!

Remember who the crowd was that Jesus was speaking to, because it was to these tax collectors, sinners, and Pharisees that had questioned the fact that He received sinners and had eaten with them. It was to this group of people that Jesus told this story. And it was equally important as we shall see that He didn't miss out the elder brother part of the story as this was very relevant to them.

It's possible that the elder brother had heard the news of his younger brother's return from one of the servants. And maybe they had filled him in with information of the sordid past that his brother had slipped into. It was the party and welcome back that enraged the elder brother!

First of all, let's consider the reason for the elder brother's anger.

He was informed that the reason for the music and party was a welcome home party for his younger brother. His reaction was a refusal point blank to go into the party, although his father came out to try and reason with him and actually pleaded with him to come to the party. But there was no convincing him; his anger was fueled by the fact that for many years he had served his father, he had obeyed the rules his father had laid down, and yet no party had ever been thrown in his honor. And then his younger brother returns from a life of reckless and extravagant sin, spending his inheritance money on prostitutes, and the fatted calf was brought out for him!

With simply natural reasoning, it doesn't seem fair at all, and it's easy to understand the elder brother's anger and stubbornness as to why he wouldn't join the party. All the pleading of his father was to no avail. The elder brother was not to be convinced. Can you imagine the outburst of the elder brother as he heard the music and got the news that his arrogant younger brother, who had brought shame upon himself, and the family, apart from wasting all his money on some of the worst sins imaginable, had returned home? His younger brother, who had fallen off the moral radar, and ended up feeding pigs, and yet the moment he arrives home, there is a huge party!

So now Jesus has set the scene. He presents his hearers with two extremes. One is that of a son who breaks every rule his father had taught him, had left home ungrateful for his upbringing, had jumped headlong into sin and debauchery, and wasted his inheritance. He seems to get the red carpet treatment and a party next to none thrown in, with a loving father gloating over him and embracing him. The other extreme is the elder brother who has stayed at home and worked on the farm, obeyed the rules, and complains that he had never had a party!

To the Pharisees, who had placed so much on the keeping of the law as the way to gain favor with God and to eternal life, this was a complete reversal of their teaching.

This really must have thrown their minds into a spin. They had never heard this before! Bad behavior almost seemed to be rewarded with a welcome home party and good behavior left outside the party! When the grace of God is removed, all we are left with is a merit system, based on good behavior or good works. The lesson Jesus was teaching was that the gospel He had come to proclaim was "good news" for all sinners, and that message is relevant to all because we are all sinners (Romans 3:23).

The pharisaical mind was unveiled in another story Jesus told in Luke 18:10–14. He told of two men who went to the temple to pray, one being a Pharisee and the other a tax collector. The Pharisee's prayer was full of self-righteousness and pride, as he compared himself to be much better than the men who were extortionists, unjust, adulterers, or even like the tax collector who was near to him. He also gloated in the fact that he fasted twice a week and paid tithes. His prayer stunk of absolute pride!

On the other hand, when the tax collector prayed, with his head bowed, he began to beat his breast asking God to be merciful to him as a sinner. In the tax collector's prayer, there was no trace of pride but an acknowledgment of his sin and unworthiness. As Jesus concluded this story, He simply said the tax collector went down to his house justified rather than the other. He then continued to press home the truth that everyone who exalts himself will be humbled, and he who humbles himself will be exalted.

Again this was so different from the way that the Pharisees had been taught.

As we return to the other prodigal son—the elder brother—can you imagine what would have happened if he had met the younger son on his way home, before his father did? Perhaps he would never have made it home; maybe he would have been turned back by the unforgiving hateful attitude of the second prodigal! One could imagine the elder son giving his brother a real dressing down and a piece of his mind, and then asking the question, "Where do you think you are going?" If that had been the case, there would have been no welcome home from the father and no party, and the father would have never had the joy of receiving his son back into the family.

It's a sad fact that many returning prodigals have been stopped on the journey by other prodigals that have supposedly kept the rules. Allow me to illustrate this point because this has been played out time and again, unfortunately, in many churches. Picture the scenario of a young man who had completely gone off the rails morally. He has rebelled against God and his upbringing, and all that he had been taught and like the prodigal had gone from one wild party to another. He had slept around, and you name it and he'd done it! He left the church looking like a clean living young man, who you would never have imagined even thinking the things that he eventually got mixed up in. Years later, he's hit rock bottom and comes to his senses and returns with much trepidation to the church family that he walked out on years before. Now the real compassionate Bible-believing church and community of Christians may not literally throw a party, but there would be a wonderful welcome. Help would be offered to get him back on his feet and established again in Christian faith. This kind of church would be filled with people who, as the Bible encourages, would weep with those who weep and rejoice with those who rejoice. The arms of love and welcome would offer him a meal, clothes, and whatever else they could help him with so that he wouldn't be left feeling second class to anyone.

Unfortunately, there are some modern Pharisees that attend churches who are hypocrites. The meaning of the word *hypocrite* is basically a "play actor."

I have often said to our grandkids when they are watching a movie, "This is not real, you know. They are only play acting. It's a movie."

They would turn around and say, "We know, Poppa. You don't need to tell us!"

But I feel I should tell you that Pharisees still exist. They look like anyone else, but their hearts are not in line with the revealed will of God.

I heard a true story of a large church in the UK that some years ago launched an outreach into their city. They had been praying for some time for the Lord to show them how they could reach more people with the gospel. The pastor had the idea of launching bus evangelism. By this, I mean they would hire coaches and pick up people from different parts of the city, where the people found difficulty in getting public bus services to the church on Sundays. Please keep in mind that the church people had been praying for new people to come into the church, for many months. Sure enough the plan worked, and new people started to attend. But one Sunday morning, the husband of one family that had been attending that church for quite a while asked if he could have a quick word with the pastor. He knew the pastor would be busy as it was just before the Sunday morning service was to begin. The pastor listened intently as he asked if he the pastor could go over to the family who were sitting on a particular row in the sanctuary and ask them to move, as they were sitting in the seats that they always sat in! The pastor looked over at the family, and there was the husband and wife and their four children. He said there they sat waiting for the meeting to begin, and he noticed the rippling muscles, tattoos, and nose ring, and this was just the wife! (I'm sure there was just a little of pastoral exaggeration in this description.) But he said to the one who had made the request, "Listen, I'll tell you what to do. You go over and ask them to move, and I promise I will give you a good funeral!"

How sad when supposed believers act in such a way that they turn people away from the church. These are prodigals who are not lost to the world, but they are elder brothers who unfortunately have no compassion and no understanding of grace, who over the years have done much harm to the kingdom of God and to people who would have been restored. It's not always the extreme actions like I have just depicted, but sometimes it is just a look or just a refusal to shake hands under the guise of having to rush off to do something else. It's the person that turns around during a church service when someone's baby is crying and gives the kind of look that says "you should keep that child quiet or take it out!" That is the kind of thing that sends people away rather than draws them in. I have come to the conclusion that many believers should read the story of the prodigal son again, and consider the truths that Jesus taught.

I also heard a true story of another church that began evangelizing their community. Some of the church people went into bars, and some gave out invitations in a local brothel. The following Sunday, one of the prostitutes came walking down the aisle with a very short skirt on; obviously, this caused quite a stir in the church as the young woman walked to the front row of the church and sat down ready for the service to begin. That morning, she heard the gospel and got wonderfully saved. She went back to her boss and told him what had happened and witnessed to some of the girls. The following Sunday, her boss came and some of the girls. Now there was an even bigger stir in the church! Later that following week, the pastor got a phone call from the young woman, although he was not used to getting phone calls from prostitutes! She told him she would be giving up her job and that she had been reading the Bible and discovered that if she would seek first the kingdom of God and His righteousness, then all the things the she would be in need of the Lord promised to supply. The pastor was amazed at the revelation this young woman had received, in just a short time since her conversion. Some of the other young women began attending the church and came to know the Lord too. But there was one old lady who came to the pastor to complain after a few weeks and said, "Pastor, these people are ruining our church."

The Pastor waited a moment and then said to the old lady, "Instead of thinking about what these girls have done, and where they have come from, why not think about what they can become? If only I can find people who could really encourage them and help them. Why don't you think about becoming one who could help them?" The old lady had never thought this way, and after a long silence, and it almost seemed like the angels of heaven were waiting with bated breath for her answer, she finally said, "You're right, Pastor. I will help to mentor them."

Everyone can change; none are above the possibility of change if only they will allow the Holy Spirit to reveal the heart of a compassionate loving heavenly Father.

The pastoral leadership changed in one church and so did the way the meetings were conducted. The music was louder, and other things seemed to have changed considerably. Many young people started to attend, but in the crowd every Sunday morning were two old ladies both in their nineties. Someone asked them the question as to how they were dealing with the changes in the church. Their answer was, "We've been praying for young people to come into this church for many years and now they are here. We regard this as an answer to prayer. What a great attitude! Too often we tend to look at things from the perspective of how they affect us rather than the bigger picture of the effect on others."

I in no way want to put off prodigals from returning to church but rather to help everyone to recognize that wherever there are hypocrites who may have the elder brother attitude, there are those who genuinely are ready to help and welcome home the lost sons and daughters. Don't let the so-called prodigal believers turn you away!

Let's take a little deeper look at the problem with the elder brother. As already mentioned, to the natural reasoning, what happened seemed unfair, and it seemed that the behavior of the younger son as bad as it was gets rewarded.

The great truth of the Bible, and the gospel Jesus proclaimed, is that our acceptance with God is based upon His grace and His grace alone. It is not that good people go to heaven and bad people go to hell; that is the big lie that has been perpetrated by the devil over the centuries. The sad thing is that many churches and preachers have helped spread this heresy and succeeded in deceiving millions into thinking that favor with God and entrance to heaven one day is based on a merit system of good works!

In normal family life as parents deal with children, this is the golden rule; children get rewarded for good behavior, and that plays out in many ways through life. In secular work, if the employee does a good job and is conscientious, he or she is a candidate for promotion and for the reward of a pay raise. If someone breaks the law and is sent to prison, it is often said when they are finally released that he or she has paid their debt to society. That is what the law demands, and that is accepted in the culture we live in. We would find it absurd and wrong if some judge after finding a person guilty of some terrible crime would pardon the criminal and set him free! There would be uproar in the media; it would be "breaking news" on TV news stations. So it only seems reasonable that we would apply this same principle to gaining favor with God. And therein lies the problem, and the thinking that is engraved into our minds that favor with God can only be gained by works.

As a young boy, I was taught the very same thing by my parents. It seemed very reasonable to me; it seemed to make sense until I heard the gospel preached and came to understand that I too was a sinner! With that said, I can fully understand the elder brother's anger, disgust, and refusal to attend the party. He had resented his younger brother's actions when he left home and more so when he finally learned the kind of lifestyle he had pursued. But I have called him the second prodigal because he missed the whole point of "grace," and this is the truth Jesus was illustrating. Every other religion demands a merit system of some kind. Christianity stands alone with the message of grace, which is God's unearned favor.

The reason why so many fail to see this truth in a modern society is because they don't understand the great plan of God in salvation. I have had various people from certain cults over the years who have tried to convince me of the opposite, with their particular message. Some have tried to tell me that no one can really be assured of eternal life, and others have told me that I must keep the Ten Commandments to attain eternal life. Let's just consider these two teachings for a moment. Wouldn't it be sad to think that a god who created all things, and went to the extreme of sending His Son into this world, who eventually was crucified, and then rose again, would ask us to believe and yet offer us no assurance of eternal life? Where would that leave us? It would leave us in "hope so" land; we would be miserable people not knowing that when death finally catches up with us that we would actually make it the courts of heaven! What an existence that would be, and existence is probably the right word, because we would be far removed from the abundant life Jesus promised His followers. We would also be so far from the experience of those early Christians who wrote as the Apostle John did regarding the truth of assurance.

"These things I have written to you who believe in the name of the Son of God, that you may know that you have eternal life, and that you may continue to believe in the name of the Son of God" (John 5:13).

Paul's' teaching of the believer's assurance is also positive, clear, and unwavering when he wrote things like "we know that when our body dies we have a building from God (another body) not made with hands eternal in the heavens" (2 Corinthians 5:1). He also uses the word "confident" that when believers are absent from the body, they are present with the Lord (2 Corinthians 5:8).

There are many other scriptures that could be mentioned along this same theme, but be assured that the Bible teaches we can be and should be assured!

The teaching that demands that we must "keep the Ten Commandments" to gain eternal life leaves us condemned. Consider the first one alone that demands that we love God with all our heart, soul, mind, and strength and have no other gods before Him. All stand guilty of breaking that one! The Bible calls it sin to break even one commandment, and we have all broken many. Paul clearly teaches, "We have all sinned and fallen short of the glory of God" (Romans 3:23).

The elder brother's attitude shows us several things. First of all, he didn't understand grace. He couldn't understand how his father could actually roll out the red carpet for a miserable sinner, who had just crawled out of the gutter of life and decided to come home! But grace doesn't look for merit points; there aren't any! That is what the good news is all about. The Bible is a revelation of the extreme love that the Father has for lost mankind. When anyone finds it difficult to accept the deepest dyed sinner can step into the kingdom of God and His favor, they have failed to grasp the whole purpose of God and what His grace is.

Secondly, the elder brother lived a life of comparisons. All the time his brother was away from home, he was probably commending himself for staying at home and working on the farm. He may have even thought that there would come a day when a greater reward would come, although he like his brother had been given his inheritance, but we are not told that he had done anything with it, and yet he still complains that no party had been thrown for him! He may have felt that his father would probably give him a double portion for his labors one day but in all of this grace didn't figure out in his thinking.

140

The problem with elder brother prodigals that attended church week by week is that it's difficult for them to accept that prodigal sons and daughters can be welcomed with a party of grace, from God the Father. They, like the elder brother, compare themselves with others and pride themselves on keeping their hands clean from the sins of the world. Their hands may be clean so to speak, but their hearts aren't; they are empty of the vital commodity of grace, forgiveness, and love.

In the prayer Jesus used to illustrate to His disciples the principles they should use when praying, he included the line that says, "Forgive us our sins as we forgive those who sin against us" (Luke 11:4). The ones who are forgiven are to forgive, and the ones who have received grace are the ones who should also show grace.

Unlearning things is often harder than learning. When someone who has been steeped in thinking all their lives that works is the way to favor with God, grace comes as a shock to their spiritual understanding. Every believer must constantly take a rain check on how we treat others, and we must make sure we are established in the love of God.

The Apostle Paul when writing to the church in the city of Ephesus wrote down a prayer that he prayed for these believers who had been miraculously saved from idolatry and the occult. It was, "That Christ may dwell in your hearts through faith; that you being rooted and grounded in love, may be able to comprehend with all the saints (believers), what is the width and length, and depth and height, to know the love of Christ which passes knowledge, that you may be filled with all the fullness of God" (Ephesians 3:17–19).

There are two words I want to draw your attention to from these scriptures. The first one is the word "rooted." It means the leafless underground part of the plant which absorbs water and minerals, stores food, and keeps the plant in place. In every believer's life, there should be a depth of spirituality that absorbs the truth of the love of God, until that truth flows out to others and at the same time keeps the believer rooted, steadfast, unmovable, and in a place where the love and grace of God becomes evident to all.

The other word is the word "know." Paul prayed that they might "know" the love of Christ. If we don't really experience His love, then all we have is head knowledge. The sad thing is that many believers slip into a knowledge of the Word of God but too often miss the experience of His love. We should seek to pour out our love to Him and allow Him to pour out His love upon us. Those times are invaluable; they are connecting times. I understand that the Bible teaches us that we are to walk by faith, but that doesn't mean we should be devoid of feelings. The love of God is not just a theological truth but a divine experience that we should seek continually. Those moments when God's presence and love are felt are life changing. They are the moments when tears of gratitude to God roll down our cheeks, and suddenly one is humbled again in the presence of the lover of our souls. I remember years ago in Bible college one of the students used to play his guitar and sing about the "lover of his soul"; the words were:

> I'm in love deeply in love with the lover of my soul,
>> I will sing praise to the King while the years of eternity roll,
>> His love is in my heart, never to depart, His blood has made me whole,
>> I'm in love with Jesus He's the lover of my soul.

The Apostle Paul wrote to the churches of Galatia, and in the opening verses of his letter writes, "I marvel that you are turning away so soon from him who called you in the grace of Christ to a different gospel, which is not another; but there are some who trouble you and want to pervert the Gospel of Christ. But even if we or an angel from heaven, preach any other gospel to you than what we have preached to you, let him be accursed. As we have said before, so now I say again, if anyone preaches any other gospel to you than what you have received, let him be accursed" (Galatians 1:6–9).

That's a pretty stern warning from the great apostle! These churches were in grave danger from false teachers of slipping back into legalism and the keeping of the law as a means of justification or acceptance with God. Paul had a hand in starting these churches on his first missionary journey to Asia Minor. He had a very close relationship with them and so feels at liberty to write very forcefully to them, of the danger they were in, by substituting legalism for the grace of God. Please note that he says there is only one gospel. It is the gospel of the grace of God. Any other teaching that denies this truth actually perverts the gospel of Christ. Please note Ephesians 2:8–9, "For by grace are you saved through faith and that not of yourselves; it is the grace of God not of works lest anyone should boast."

The problem with the elder brother was that he was devoid of this grace; he didn't appreciate the love of his father and had lived his life with a servant attitude comparing himself with others. He didn't see the privileges of sonship, and neither did he recognize that the Father's blessing was the Father's prerogative to give. It's a cold uncertain religious world to live in when anyone lives outside of the revelation of the grace of God.

It reminds me of a parable or story Jesus told recorded in Matthew 20. It is called the parable of the workers in the vineyard. The owner had agreed with the workers that they would be paid a denarius per day. After he had set them to work, he went and hired others who started work at the third hour of the day; he did this again at the sixth hour and the eleventh hour. The story goes on to tell us that when the day's work was finished, the ones who had started late got exactly the same amount as those who had worked all day! Of course at first glance, one can understand the workers who had worked all day complaining as they did, but the argument the owner used was simple. Basically he was saying to them, "We agreed on a set amount, and that is what you received, and what I want to give to the late starters is my prerogative!"

This story is set against the backdrop of Peter's question in Matthew 18:27. "See we have left all and followed you so what will we have?" Jesus had just been teaching on how hard it is for a rich man to enter the kingdom of God, and Peter was making a comparison between those who have riches and don't feel the need of God and him and the disciples who had forsaken all. Of course, there will be rewards for faithful service in heaven one day, but the whole point of the parable was any reward given is the owner of the vineyard's decision, and all the workers were working at His invitation. If the Lord one day wants to give those who come to repentance and the knowledge of eternal life towards the end of their earthly life the same reward as those who have labored for him for many years, then who are we to argue? The recipients of the grace of God should be satisfied that they are recipients, because without the grace of God we would all be lost with no hope of eternal life! We all have to remember whatever we have done in labors for the Lord, it is all because of His grace. The Apostle Paul said, "By the grace of God I am what I am, and His grace toward me was not in vain, but I labored more abundantly than they all yet not I but the grace of God which was with me" (1 Corinthians 15:10).

The Apostle John when writing of Jesus said, "We beheld Him full of grace and truth" (John 1:14). If He had just been full of "truth," that would have condemned us as we are all sinners, but He was full of grace and truth. By God's grace, his divine favor is extended to us even though we are guilty.

The story is told of a certain man who got to the gates of heaven, and there was Peter standing at the gate. I repeat. It is a story not a biblical story. The man was looking to enter only to hear Peter tell him that he needed one hundred points to be allowed access.

The man thought for a moment and said, "I have always been faithful to my wife."

Peter said, "That's three points."

"I have read the Bible several times."

Peter said, "That's another two points."

The man realized this was going to be really hard, so he mentioned he had served in a soup kitchen for the poor, he had attended church, he had given money to charity, and as many other things he could possibly think of, and his total score was only in the twenties.

The man looked at Peter and said, "The only way I'm going to make it into heaven is by the grace of God."

Peter said, "That's worth one hundred points. Go ahead. Enter!"

We may smile at such a story, but the truth is nothing outside of God's grace is good enough, and the only reason God can offer grace is because Jesus Christ paid the debt of sin we owed when He died upon the cross.

It was grace that said to the woman who was caught in the act of adultery "Neither do I condemn you, go and sin no more" (John 8:11).

It was grace that brought salvation to the tax collector Zacchaeus, after he had stolen from so many.

It was grace that arrested Saul of Tarsus and changed him into the Apostle Paul (Acts 9). It is the grace of God that is waiting for all prodigals with a party all prepared.

The elder brother made his thoughts known to his father, only to hear the words, "Son you are always with me, and all that I have is yours. It was right that we should make merry and be glad, for your brother was dead and is alive again and was lost and is found." It was right! Grace is always right, but the elder brother had lived without availing himself of the privileges of his father's house. He was living and serving on his father's farm without enjoying all the privileges that were his. When believers simply serve without enjoying the privileges of sonship, they become judgmental and devoid of forgiveness, the joy of the Lord, and the grace of God.

The sad thing in this story is that we do not read that the elder brother went into the party! To the Pharisees who were listening to this story told by Jesus, it would seem that the brother who had lived a reckless and extravagant lifestyle got rewarded, and the one who stayed at home and kept his hands clean missed out! Jesus ended the story there purposefully to press this truth home to those who were listening, whose belief system was similar to the one the Galatians were in danger of being drawn back into.

When we live without enjoying and living in the grace of God, we are left with a cold religion that becomes a set of rules and regulations. Serving becomes a chore not an enjoyment. The elder brother would go to his bed at the end of the day having done another day's work, but in all the days of his labors, he never enjoyed a party or availed himself of all the family privileges.

In the story recorded in Luke 10:38–42, that of the two sisters Mary and Martha, it was Martha who had welcomed Jesus into her house; her sister Mary was the one who sat at Jesus's feet listening to His teaching. While all this was taking place, Martha was in the kitchen preparing food and serving her guests. She complained to Jesus and asked Him if He thought it was fair that she did all the serving, while her sister had left her in order to listen to His words. She actually asked Jesus to tell Mary that she should come and help her. It is interesting what the answer Jesus gave. He said, "Martha, Martha, you are troubled about many things," but one thing is needed or really important and Mary has chosen this, and what she has received will never be taken away from her. What Martha did was obviously needed; she was concerned with the practical things of preparing food, and what Mary was doing by sitting at Jesus's feet was also needed. Both should blend together. The Father looks and seeks for worshipers (John 4:23), and He also needs workers for the harvest field (Matthew 9:37–38).

The elder brother had been busy serving but never enjoyed the privileges of His father's grace and love. Charles Spurgeon said, "You must go with Martha but first sit with Mary." Serving the Lord should spring out of an intimate relationship with Him where His Word and presence inspire you to do His will. Local churches would not operate the way they should if they had people who just came to worship; all the many tasks and ministries that are needed to minister to people of all ages need worshipers who are servants!

Many so-called Christians attend church week by week, out of routine. They clock watch, and they are glad to get out of the place as soon as the closing prayer has been made. It reminds me of when I was at school, we would all watch the clock ready for the bell to ring and school day was finished. We could then rush outside and get on with things that to us were a lot more enjoyable. When the summer recess was near, we couldn't wait for six weeks without school! In the last day, we would be willing for the clock to go faster, and when finally we were let out of school, we would go shouting across the playground, "No more school, no more stick, no more silly arithmetic!" (by stick I mean a cane as in those in days if we didn't behave or did badly with our work the teacher or headmaster would cane us on the hands or the backside); we were glad to be away for six whole weeks!

When people become reluctant to attend church and start making excuses as to why they can't be there each week, there is a problem. And it may be that they have left themselves outside the party!

If that describes you, take a fresh look at the grace of God and the privileges that the Lord extends to all who really love Him. It was difficult and humbling for the younger brother to return after all he had done, but he did return, and he did walk right into a party.

It's difficult sometimes for the "elder brother prodigals" who somehow have missed the excitement of Father's lavish love and blessings. The elder brother missed the party; he was too judgmental and void of the understanding of grace. It may be humbling to apologize for a wrong attitude and to throw your arms around a returning prodigal, but whatever it takes, don't miss the party.

And please remember, "there is always a way back."

Chapter 18

Restoration of Wasted Years

The amazing grace of God is portrayed in this story of the prodigal son, but the Bible gives us a further revelation of God's goodness, and that is that all the wasted years that may have been given to living in ways that were not pleasing to God, He is willing and able to restore (Joel 2:25). That has to be great news for every one of us.

The above verse may seem a little strange, but allow me to give you a little background which hopefully will help you to understand what exactly the Prophet Joel is saying to the nation of Judah. Joel has been called the prophet of religious revival; he knew that revival follows repentance. The land of Israel had just suffered a terrible plague of locusts. These locusts had devoured every green thing; whenever locusts went through a land, they left a trail of destruction in their path.

Judah had gone through a terrible famine which was caused by the plague of locusts that had eaten up all vegetation and crops. The people had also suffered a prolonged drought, and the land was in utter devastation, with flocks and people dying. The picture was simply one of carnage destruction and death. And like the prodigal who also suffered from the effects of famine which eventually brought him to his senses, Judah had also fallen into sin and a backslidden state, and the swarm of locusts that wrought destruction was the judgment of God upon the land. A plague of locusts could leave a vineyard stripped of its leaves, and its branches left bare and white within a matter of minutes.

This plague of locusts is called a great army, and some interpreters view this as an army that is to come in the last days, and while prophecy can sometimes have a double application, I tend to think that this is referring to an actual swarm of locusts that had ravaged the land.

Take note of Joel 1:4, "What the chewing locust left, the crawling locust has eaten; and what the crawling locust left, the consuming locust has eaten."

Also, Joel 1:17 gives a vivid description of the land. "The seed shrivels under the clods. Storehouses are in shambles; barns are broken down, for the grain has withered."

Drunkards felt the effects of this devastation, because the vines had been destroyed (Joel 1:5).

Priests had no meat offerings or drink offerings of wine to offer; the vines had been destroyed, and so had the grain and the cattle were dying (Joel 1:9).

Cattle and sheep cried out in the fields (Joel 1:20).

Everyone was affected by the onslaught of this terrible army! But the Prophet Joel had a message of hope. He first called the people to repentance but then promised them that God could restore to them, and not only restore but make up to them the years they had lost and had been wasted through this destruction!

Wasted years, and wasted time, and as the saying goes, "time waits for no man."

Everyone looks back at some point in their life and possibly wishes they could roll the years back and use them more profitably. There can be lapses in commitment to the cause of Christ from believers for a number of reasons, e.g., the pressures of work and bringing up a family, and while these things can and should be balanced out with our day-to-day walk with the Lord, the truth is that so often they are not. As I have mentioned earlier in the book, "prodigals are not just the ones that leave and go headlong into extravagant and reckless sin." They can attend church week by week and be there in body but not in spirit. Their priorities have drifted to other things, but to all intents and purposes, they look like the rest and sit in their usual seat; they shake hands and greet people with a smile. But deep down, they are allowing the enemy of apathy to drain them of valuable years.

The question that needs to be answered by everyone who reads this book is, "Are there times be they months or years that you feel have been wasted?"

We are not told how long the prodigal son had been away from home, but that is not the important thing. What is important is that he came back home and in so doing discovered "there is always a way back."

Many people live with regret as they look back over their lives. It is a truly wonderful place to be in when we can say at the end of our lives as the Apostle Paul did, "I have fought the good fight, I have finished the race, I have kept the faith. Finally there is laid up for me the crown of righteousness, which the righteous judge, will give me on that day, and not to me only but also to all who have loved His appearing" (2 Timothy 4:7–8).

These words were penned when Paul was nearing execution, yet he could look back on a life since his conversion, where he had never been disobedient to the heavenly vision the Lord had given him and the ministry he had been called to.

I remember my dad would say to me when I was just a young boy that time seems to fly by when you get older. Of course, like many kids when they hear things like that, it really doesn't register. Getting older seems way too far in the future to even give it a second thought, and yet now I understand the years seem to come and go so quickly. But the promise we are considering from the Prophet Joel gives everyone hope and a reason to take heart—even if there are some wasted years and regrets. God can miraculously restore what we lost in those wasted years, but before we consider this, allow me to give a few examples that may have caused us regret and have been responsible for the wasted years.

The Wasted Years of Addictions

Addictions are a commonplace in our culture today. The definition of the word *addiction* is "the state of being enslaved to a habit or practice or to something that is psychologically or physically habit forming." Addictions lead a person down the path to depression and enslave a person until they become desperate for more of the same. The problem is that more of the same only feeds the addiction which is never satisfied. As stated earlier in this book, it's so often the loneliness of the soul is seeking fulfillment and connection, but when the search ends in addictions, it can often leave us in the mire of depression.

To the inner hurts, loneliness of soul, and ensuing problems, the enemy will tempt you with the things that offer to blur and mask the real problems. The ultimate answer lies in finding the way back to the Father's presence, but the devil will never lead anyone in that direction! Rather, he will seek to turn them to what seems a quick fix, but never is. It only leads to more of the accompanying problems that addictions bring. Addictions can take on many different forms; some of the common ones are of course drugs, alcoholism, pornography, lust, and sexual addictions. The addiction becomes the driving force which enslaves the mind and in turn controls the actions and way of life of the person caught in their snare. The addiction becomes a false god and takes its place as the number one priority in the life of the addict, driving them to the next so-called fix! These things take their toll on the human body and mind and waste years and sometimes lives if they are not rescued in time.

The Wasted Years of Immorality

This, of course, is nothing new; it's been prevalent from the beginnings of time. We see the rampant gross sin of the cities of Sodom and Gomorrah in Abraham's time. In Genesis 19:4–5, we have the account of two angels that had gone into the city of Sodom, and Lot Abraham's nephew took them into his house. We are told that the men of the city and the men of Sodom both old and young and all the people from every quarter surrounded the house and called out to Lot and said to him, "Where are the men who came to you tonight? Bring them out to us that we may know them carnally." These sexual sins were not hidden but rather were the culture of that city, there was no apparent shame, and this seems to have become so culturally acceptable at that time that young and old engaged in these things. What we now see increasingly across our culture is a huge swing back to the acceptance of such things under the guise of political correctness.

What may be called political correctness by a modern society is defiance toward the moral laws of God. Biblical guidelines and principles have been erased by our modern culture. It's almost as if someone has taken a white board and written the moral laws of God on it and then taken a cloth eraser and wiped the board clean! Once we take God out of the equation and His laws, we have no rules. Everyone then does what is right in their own eyes, which leads to absolute chaos. Fornication or pre-marital sex and also extra-marital sex (adultery) are now a commonplace in our society. We seem to have hit an all-time high of sexual misconduct with accusations coming almost every day against high-profile people. These among many other things are the modern-day addictions that seek to destroy the lives of men and women. These are the locusts that have stolen and wasted the years of so many, leaving them devoid and stripped of the life and purposes of God. The problem today is that the lines of demarcation between the world and the church with these issues have become very fuzzy.

The Wasted Years of Pornography

The computer is a great tool for many things when used correctly, but it can also become the doorway to secret sin. Pornography lures people into its trap of addiction and then fills them with guilt and the fear of being caught. In the process, this locust robs the addict of peace and self-respect. These things are not written to heap guilt upon any who are struggling with addictions, but rather to show that as you discover "there is always a way back," there is also a promise of restoration for wasted years.

There Are the Wasted Years of Not Enough Time for the Family

It is said that no one says on their deathbed, "I wish I had spent more time at the office." The problem is that many fall into the trap of financial debt and burdens as a result of huge mortgages, car payments, etc. The strain and stress of financial burdens create huge time restraints on family life, and relationships suffer. And valuable time with children is lost. Opportunities pass by so fast, and Harry Chapin in "Cat's in the Cradle" seems to capture this in a song about a boy who asked his father every day if he would spend time with him. His father was a busy man, and the song takes us from toddler to college days.

> "When you comin' home Dad?"
> "I don't know when
> but we'll get together then
> you know we'll get together then"

> Well he came from college just the other day,
> so much like a man I just had to say,
> "Son, I'm proud of you, can you sit for a while?"
> He shook his head and said with a smile
> "What I'd really like, Dad, is to borrow the car keys,
> see you later, can I have them please?"

> "When you comin' home, Son?"
> "I don't know when,
> but we'll get together then,
> you know, we'll have a good time then"

It's not only children that can suffer, but the relationship of husband and wife can also be stretched to a breaking point. Financial pressures bring stress, and far too often, communication lines are broken through the busyness of trying to make ends meet. Why do we do it? Why do we allow things that are of lesser importance to rob of the most important? Arguments ensue because of pressure; romance becomes something of the past, and before too long the temptation of either husband or wife is to look elsewhere and seek the affections of another. These things just lead to wasted years as we have allowed the hungry locust to devour what is of primary importance.

The Wasted Years of Shattered Dreams

Shattered dreams are all that some people have left. We all know that in the kind of world we live in, dreams can easily be shattered. We all start out in life with some kind of dreams, some of course bigger than others. Not every entrepreneur makes it in business; everyone doesn't always get the grades they aimed for or the promotion at work. Everyone deep down wants to be a success; no one likes failure, but some succeed, and others don't. The happy marriage that started out with all the potential may have ended in the divorce court, and you feel like you are just another statistic, and the bottom of your world has dropped out. Instead of a dream coming true, it turned out to be a nightmare. It almost seems that it has been an attack from hell, and actually it has. The locust of destruction has been at work.

There are many other scenarios that one could mention that we are all familiar with, but as in the prophecy of Joel, the locusts came to destroy, so demonic spirits have the same mission. And you may have been on the receiving end, but God always has the last word in every situation, and he says to you today, "I can restore the years the locusts have eaten."

The Wasted Years of Aborted Ministry

Allow me for a brief moment to apply this to the pastors and preachers who have been involved or are involved in ministry. Sometimes preachers look back on wasted years. The stress of ministry can take its toll. Statistics tell us that many quit the ministry

154

year by year. In 2017, it was reported that 1,700 leave the ministry each month. Some have fallen sadly to immoral sins and have to quit the ministry, but the main reasons most leave the ministry are the demands and challenges of modern ministry. Some feel underpaid and overworked. Others leave due to the general lack of real commitment within the church community and the western-style approach to Christianity, which so often falls short of the New Testament church. People come visiting churches just to check them out and see what facilities they have to offer. Others leave after being attendees for months or possibly years, without a word of explanation, and pastors are left wondering if integrity still exists. Loneliness can also be a problem in ministry. It shouldn't be, but it can be. There are sometimes no close friends with whom a pastor can confide with, as to how he is really feeling. This in turn can lead to depression and frustration. The highest calling anyone can receive that of the calling to the ministry can be aborted and walked away from, and the pastor looks back with sadness on what seems to be wasted years.

The pastor of any church needs to be covered in prayer by those who stand with him, as he is a target of the enemy constantly. Let us consider all the things that the great Apostle Paul endured for the sake of the gospel, such as shipwrecks, beatings, imprisonment, stoning, and perils of robbers, and that is apart from some of the churches that turned against him, plus dealing with false teachers, and problems within some of the churches. I am encouraged to know that he could say at the end of his ministry that he had not been disobedient to the heavenly vision that the Lord had given to him at the moment of conversion (Acts 26:19).

I am thankful to the Lord that over the years the Lord has, by His grace, sustained me even in the deepest valleys and trials that every pastor goes through. Although I have painted perhaps a negative picture of the ministry, I must also write of the many believers over the years that have stood with us, prayed us through, encouraged us, and blessed us beyond words. Charles H. Spurgeon once said, "If God calls you to the ministry don't stoop to be a King." I have never regretted my call and never doubted it and wouldn't change it, but I too look back over the years and like so many have to ask the question as to whether I could have done better and been more effective. But to every minister who reads this, whatever happened along the journey, let me encourage you. He knows everything you have gone through, and He is ready to restore the years that the locusts have eaten and that you may feel have been wasted.

Now let's consider how God can do this. The prophecy and promise from Joel was given to a people who had come under severe judgment; as already mentioned, the land had been devastated, and when there is a plague of locusts followed by famine, everyone suffers! The healing and restoration of the land as already stated in a previous chapter relative to the promise that God gave to Solomon would depend upon Israel's repentance, humility, and of course, prayer (2 Chronicles 7:14). Nevertheless, the promise was restoration and healing. The little word that precedes this is the word *if*—*if* my people will pray. Restoration waits upon our response.

Joel calls the people to consecration.

> Blow the trumpet in Zion, consecrate a fast. Call a sacred assembly; gather the people sanctify the congregation. Assemble the elders; gather the children and nursing babes. Let the bridegroom go out from his chamber and the bride from her dressing room. Let the priests who minister to the Lord, weep between the porch and the altar. Let them say, "Spare your people, O Lord, and do not give your heritage to reproach, that the nations should rule over them. Why should they say among the peoples, Where is their God?" Then the Lord will be jealous for His land and pity His people.
>
> (Joel 2:15–18)

In the story of the prodigal son, the turning point was when he turned back toward home and walked the path of humility. The welcome back and forgiveness, along with the party of celebration and restoration to the family, all followed on the heels of his response.

The restoration of wasted years also follows the response of every individual who in one way or another feels they have some wasted years along their journey.

Please note several things Joel called the nation to as he urged them to respond and believe for restoration.

The blowing of the trumpet was a clarion call to consecration. The trumpet was blown for various reasons, sometimes to call the people to battle and among other things also the times when they summoned the people to gather for prayer and solemn assemblies.

The priests were called to passionate intercession, the kind of intercession that is accompanied with tears.

God, who is always waiting, longing, preparing, and working behind the scenes to bring home prodigals, is the god who can turn things around and order restoration.

The Bible is full of accounts when God stepped in and miraculously ordered events so that there was a complete turnaround. Abraham and Sarah waited twenty-five years for Isaac to be born. When this actually happened, Abraham was one hundred years old and Sarah ninety! There was also a period during those twenty-five years when there seems to be no word from the Lord for thirteen years! This was after Abraham had fathered a child with his maid and had given way to fleshly unbelief in the promise of God.

Abram was eighty-six years old when Hagar bore Ishmael to Abram (Genesis 16:16).

The next verse (Genesis 17:1) is when Abram was ninety-nine years old, the Lord appeared to him, "I am the Almighty God; walk before me and be blameless . . ."

Thirteen years were possibly looked upon by Abraham as wasted years, but all that faded into the past, when God blessed them with a miracle baby called Isaac. And God showed to both Abraham and Sarah that He was the Almighty and nothing is too hard for the Lord.

Joseph waited thirteen years as a slave for the dream to be fulfilled, but God proved to him also that He never forgets His promises, and despite all the circumstances Joseph went through, God turned things around, and Joseph experienced a restoration of wasted years. Someone well said, "God prepares His leaders in a slow cooker not a microwave!"

Moses was another example of this; he spent forty years in the backside of the desert before God called him to deliver Egypt. By the way, he had then turned eighty years of age. Someone of old age when asked if they worry about their age answered, "It's just a matter of numbers!" The truth is God is not put off by old age or youth. The promise of the outpouring of the Holy Spirit in Acts 2 includes the young who will see visions and the old who will dream dreams.

While Moses had made his mistakes and got into a fight and killed an Egyptian when he was a much younger man and still in Egypt, I'm sure he looked on those wilderness years as possibly forty wasted years, although they were years of preparation for what would lay ahead. However what Moses witnessed of the miraculous workings of God in his later years, more than made up for what he may have felt had been wasted! But the god who opened prison doors and stilled the turbulent seas and the god who opened the Red Sea and the Jordan River, for His people to walk through on dry ground, is still the same today. The god who caused Jericho's walls to fall flat at the blast of the trumpets of the army of Israel, and who stopped the mouths of lions, to preserve His servant Daniel. The god who made a way in the wilderness with miracle after miracle is still the same today. He is the god of the supernatural and the god who turns things around. He is the god who can restore your wasted years with an abundance of blessing.

The Prophet Joel brings this message of hope, restoration, and abundance of blessing.

"The Lord will answer and say to His people, 'Behold I will send you grain and new wine and oil . . .'" (Joel 2:19).

Grain represents harvest and with harvest not only comes provision but prosperity. New wine is typical of rejoicing and joy, and oil is representative of the Holy Spirit.

In fact, that is not all that Joel prophesied concerning the land; please note Joel 2:23–24, "Be glad then you children of Zion, and rejoice in the Lord your God; for He has given you the former rain faithfully. And He will cause the rain to come down to you the former rain and the latter rain in the first month. The threshing floors shall be full of wheat, and the vats shall overflow with new wine and oil."

This speaks of abundance not simply restoration but an abundant restoration. That will surpass all that they missed during the wasted years.

As already stated, restoration of wasted years begins with us, and the belief that the god of the Bible who loved us enough to send his Son to die in our place is a loving heavenly Father who is described by Jesus in the story of the prodigal son. First of all, be convinced of this, and let your heart be filled with this truth. Acknowledge before the Lord where you may have failed and allow his Word and the Holy Spirit to guide you into doing what you can to bring about restoration.

For those who look back on relationships within the family who may have suffered from so many things as already mentioned, a new start is possible and a closer relationship with your spouse or children can start today. Don't wait for the other party to take the initiative. The big question with every marital problem that threatens to end in the divorce court is, "Do both husband and wife want the marriage to work?" That may sound totally elementary and in some ways it is, but whenever my wife and I are counseling any married couple, that is the first question we ask. If there is a willingness to save the marriage, then the marriage can be saved. It may take time to work through the problems and for trust to be built again, depending on what the real issue is, but if both are willing to work at it, then their marriage doesn't have to end in the divorce court, and they both can save themselves a lot of money and heartache in the process.

On the other hand, there may be relationships that may never be the same as they were; perhaps divorce has put an end to what once seemed to be a happy marriage. There may be some things we can't turn the clock back on, but we can start with making sure our heart is not entombed in bitterness, by allowing forgiveness to flow. You may be the innocent party and never wanted the marriage to end in the way it did. The one thing we should all be certain of is that no one can stop us from doing what is necessary to have a heart free from bitterness and filled with the love of God. It may be humbling to make the phone call or write the letter, but it's liberating and opens the way for a restoration of wasted years.

You may wonder what reception you will get perhaps from an estranged child. Please don't let the enemy dissuade you from trying. Pray that God will open the hearts of all those who may have been affected, and believe that we do have a god who answers prayer.

Addictions as already mentioned can enslave us, and nobody said it's an easy thing to break free. But let me encourage you it is not impossible; many have done it and some after many years. My first ever visit to the United States was to a church in Los Angeles that was made up mainly of ex-drug addicts. The pastor was himself, a former heroin addict for thirteen years, who was miraculously delivered. Hundreds of young men and women attended that church who had been delivered from addictions.

In turning to the Lord, make yourself accountable to spiritual people in a good Bible-believing church. There are people who can pray with you and programs that you can join for all kinds of addictions. But please don't give up. God is waiting for you with the promise of restoration. Let that vision fill your mind and resist every thought of condemnation that the enemy will throw at you, in order to make you feel second class. Remember this, and I say this to a group of men that I regularly minister to, who are all in a rehabilitation program because they are seeking to beat their addiction. "Your history is not your destiny." Your destiny is restoration!

The prodigal looked up that road that led to home with trepidation, but if he hadn't have walked that road, he would have missed his restoration.

For those who may fall into the category of having "shattered dreams," some of the things already mentioned may be your shattered dreams, but please understand from the ashes of failure, God can make success. Wrong choices and decisions or sometimes just circumstances that changed overnight can shatter dreams. Some people have been broken under the burden of debt; maybe it was bad money management or perhaps just the economy that took a nose dive and everything changed and you felt trapped. Many of the success stories in the business world, if you look into it, the people concerned went through times when they hit rock bottom. The only way they became a success is because they got up again and worked through it. As far as finances are concerned, I don't hold to the teaching that seems to stretch the prosperity message to an extreme. I do believe God wants to prosper us, but prosperity is not gauged by how big a car we drive or a house we live in, etc. My definition would simply be this that prosperity is having our needs met with some left over in order to bless others.

Again, there are financial stewardship programs that can help with budgets and how to handle finances. These are some of the steps we can take, but beyond all that as we put into practice the Word of God that teaches liberality and the blessing of tithing, God can indeed open the windows of the provisions of heaven to us (Malachi 3).

Aborted Ministry

For someone who feels they have failed in whatever ministry they felt the Lord call them to is an experience that no one wants to go through. Someone once said the best cure for the fear of failure is to fail. That may be true but it still hurts, especially if they feel they have let God down and in the process let people down.

Pastors always want to have big churches and look for success in that way, but real success is not measured in numbers but in faithfulness. But sometimes after being called to the greatest privilege of all that is to preach the gospel and to build the kingdom of God, the fallout rate is still too many. And the ones, who for whatever reason quit their ministry to pursue other things, can battle with guilt, failure, and the feeling of defeat. But that doesn't have to be the end of the road or your story. Failure is written on the resumé of many of the great men and women who rose to the heights of faith. There was Abraham who struggled at times with lack of faith and selfish ways, who went onto to reach a level of faith where he staggered not at the promise of God through unbelief. And he also went on to become the father of the child of promise, Isaac. Abraham became known as the "friend of God." There was David who, as mentioned earlier in the book, committed adultery and arranged the murder of Bathsheba's husband to cover his sin, and yet became known as one who served his generation by the will of God. And to mention just one more from the New Testament, there is Peter who denied three times he ever knew Jesus Christ. He, along with so many down the ages, felt the ultimate failure but rose to become a great apostle.

Your story isn't finished. Whatever is the reason for wasted years, a new day can dawn. Believe in the God of restoration. The psalmist in Psalm 108:2 declares, "I will awaken the dawn." For the prodigal, the moment his steps turned homeward, the dark night of his soul was soon to give way to the dawn of the day of restoration. The Father waits and watches because "there is always a way back."

Don Francisco wrote a song entitled "I Don't Care Where You've Been Sleeping." One of the verses says

> Although you've gone so far from Me and wasted all those years
> Even though my name's been spattered by the mire in which you lie
> I'd take you back this instant if you'd turn to Me and cry.

Chapter 19

Where Did You Come from and Where Are You Going?

That may sound a strange title for this chapter, but allow me to take you back into the Old Testament and into the story again of Abram and Sarai—or as they become better known as Abraham and Sarah, in the intervening years of Abraham having received the promise from God that he would become the father of a great nation. The promise was only fulfilled some twenty-five years later. In Genesis 16, it opens by saying that Sarai had borne Abram no children, and believing that she was too old to bear a child, she persuaded her husband Abram to have a relationship with her maid Hagar. She and Abram lapsed into unbelief regarding the promise of God. Abram listened to his wife and did as she suggested, and Hagar became pregnant. Sarai then became jealous and despised Hagar, and she began to deal harshly with her; the result was that Hagar had to flee from her presence. The story goes on to tell us that the angel of the Lord found Hagar by a spring of water in the wilderness and asked Hagar this question, "Where have you come from and where are you going?" It was not that the angel didn't know the answer before asking the question, but he simply wanted Hagar to be open and honest with her answer.

Where did you come from and where are you going is a very searching question for any of us. If the prodigal had been asked that

163

question, he would have answered differently at various stages of his life—relative to the experiences he was going through. Had he been asked that question when he had just left his father's house, his answer would have been, "I've just left home, and I'm heading for the big city many miles away." If he had been asked that question after leaving the pigsty, his answer would have been totally different. He had tasted of the dregs of sin and had a bitter taste in his mouth, and a horrible smell on his clothes, along with a heart and mind that were bereft of peace and snared with guilt. "I'm leaving the extravagant and excessive life-style of sin that eventually led to the pigsty, and I'm returning home," would have no doubt been his answer. At least the prodigal, I believe, would have been honest as the story portrays. As you have read through this book, may I be permitted to ask you the same question? The honest answer is the key to unlocking the future blessings of God and making the journey to restoration, because "there is always a way back."

Perhaps, like the prodigal of old, you can identify with some of the things mentioned in the book. Maybe you are not guilty of having reached the depths that he did; on the other hand, maybe you are. Please remember that the story Jesus told was to portray His Father's heart of love and grace.

There are many prodigals, millions of them, scattered throughout the world that have family members praying for them and churches interceding for them. There are other kinds of prodigals, as mentioned earlier in the book, many who sit in church week by week; they give worship a pass and never really attempt to sing of the greatest love story of all. Prayer to them becomes a few quick words as though it is intended to keep the relationship with God alive, just in case they need Him at some future point or crisis.

There are prodigal husbands or wives who, like the church at Ephesus, have left their first love (for each other, Revelation 2:4). This particular church was born in revival (Acts 19), and the Holy Spirit had many things to commend them for, but He was not happy; they had left their first love. Sometimes, marriages can slip into the same trap. The bills are paid, the meals are on the table, everything looks fine, but the first love has vanished. It's time to start dating again and fan back into a flame of that first love.

There are prodigal parents who have never been friends with their kids. I remember years ago a pastor realizing he hadn't spent enough time with his son and told him that he would keep Wednesday evenings free for him starting with the coming week. Wednesday came around, and the boy's dad was ready to do just what his son wanted to do with the evening he had kept free for him. "Well what shall we do tonight, son?"

His son answered, "I'm sorry, but I have arranged to play with my friends tonight."

That was the moment that his father realized he was not his son's friend!

There are those who once witnessed for Christ of their personal salvation without fear or embarrassment but have lost the passion for souls. Preachers who have veered from the truth of the challenge of the gospel and rather than preach the whole counsel of God have preached to keep people happy and have been afraid of people leaving for more comfortable, less challenging preaching. There are many things that could be mentioned, but where have you come from is not the important thing, but rather, it is where are you going?

God has His army of intercessors all over the world; they are here at home and also placed strategically in all the "far countries" prodigals can stray to. Let me encourage everyone who at this moment of time is praying for prodigals. Don't give up; keep believing. Prayer sometimes seems to be a mystery, but allow me to share just a few thoughts to encourage you because God works as we pray.

Please note James 4:2, "You do not have because you do not ask."

If we take this scripture at face value, we must conclude that some things do not happen because we do not ask. Therefore, if we ask, we can cause things to happen. In other words, we should not take the attitude that "what will be, will be," but rather what we want to be, we have to be willing to ask for. Jesus told the story of the man who had a friend who came to visit him at midnight, but the problem was his larder was empty; he had no bread to give him. However, he also had a friend across the road who he believed would have some bread. Although it was midnight, he decided to knock on his door. His friend shouted down to him that they were all in bed and his family was all asleep. Nevertheless, he continued knocking. Jesus said it was because of the man's importunity or as the NKJ version of the Bible puts it because of his persistence, his friend got up and gave him the bread he asked for. This leads us to the thought that it was his continual asking that eventually got his friend to give him the bread (Luke 11:5–10).

Jack Hayford in his book, *Prayer Is Invading the Impossible*, brings out something rather different to how this is usually interpreted. "Now answer me," Jesus is saying, "which of you has a friend who would stand at his bedroom window and shout out to you saying 'Don't bother me. The whole household's in bed'? Of course not! It's not even a question of friendship. The man will get up and give him what he needs because of the simple fact that the neighbor had the nerve to ask. And I'm telling you—ask and it shall be given to you!" That's the uncluttered version of Jesus's story. It tells how to learn to pray well. To begin, you need to learn to have the nerve to ask boldly. Hayford goes onto say, "A look at the original language supports this simple approach, so much so that it is mind boggling to understand why this passage has been used to show that prayer must earn answers through overcoming God's reluctance, as if our persistence could overcome God's resistance."

The writer of the book of Hebrews supports this in Hebrews 4:16, "Let us therefore come boldly to the throne of grace that we may obtain mercy and find grace to help in time of need." There is no hint of reluctance here on the part of God but rather the opposite. I want to encourage everyone who is praying for a prodigal to dare to believe and pray some bold prayers. Far too many believers pray for a while and then in their minds revert to the thought that God is sovereign, so if it is His will, it will happen, and instead of standing in faith, they ease up on their intercession and leave it all with the god who is sovereign!

Allow me to address this for a moment. The word sovereign really means supreme or supremacy. Now I'm sure every believer reading this book will agree that God is supreme. But let's take this thought a little further and ask what does the word "will" mean?

We also fall back onto this so many times and say, "If it is God's will, it will happen," as though we have no part to play in the whole process. The word *will* is another word for *desire*. The Apostle Peter wrote "The Lord is not slack concerning His promise, as some count slackness, but is longsuffering toward us, not willing that any should perish but that all should come to repentance" (2 Peter 3:9).

Clearly then God is not "willing" that any should perish! Of course that is true; that is the very reason He gave His Son as a sacrifice for our sins. But the truth is that some will perish even though that is not God's will! They have a free will, a choice. But as we pray for them, God's desires and our desires meet, and as we delight ourselves in the Lord, He will give us the desires of our heart, so the desires we have within our heart are the desires God has given and placed there (Psalm 37:4). Something happens as we delight ourselves in the Lord. He implants His desires into our hearts so that they too become our desires and as we pray things happen.

In the whole mystery of prayer, we have to come to understand the truth and the principles on which God works. God has always looked for an intercessor; He always looks to partner with His people. He requires us to have faith and to ask and to take up the mantle of authority that Adam lost but is now ours through Christ's victory at the cross. It is also evident that although God is "immutable," that is, unchanging as far as His character is concerned. He is perfect, and perfection does not need to change, but God can change His mind! This truth is born out in several instances in the Old Testament—I will remind you of just one when Moses was on Mount Sinai with the Lord receiving the Ten Commandments he pleaded or interceded with God not to destroy Israel because of their idolatry. They had made a golden calf in Moses's "absence," and this became the object of their worship. God was intent on destroying the nation and beginning again with Moses, but Moses interceded, and we have this amazing verse in Exodus 32:14, "So the Lord relented from the harm which he said He would do to His people." In other words, God changed His mind!

For every prodigal out there who may be a long way from home right now, let all praying parents, families, and churches believe that as you partner with God for lost souls and prodigals to return, you have been gifted with great authority in prayer. Pray boldly. The prodigals are returning!

"Where did you come from?" the angel asked Hagar, and if the same question is posed to you, only you can answer it. Where are you on the journey? Perhaps you picked this book up and you are intent on heading away to a far country so to speak. Think again; it will only lead to disaster and heartache. Perhaps you are on your way back, something is stirring in your heart again, and you really long deep down to get back in the Father's presence, with His blessing and restoration. Keep going, and remember He is waiting, preparing, and ready to run to meet you.

Maybe, like the older brother, you have never been away, but rather you have been working in the field, but where you are going is the question. The unfortunate part of the story is the elder brother never entered the party. Take another long look at the cross; see the blood-stained figure marred more than any man. Hear His prayer for forgiveness for those who had crucified Him. Allow the Holy Spirit to melt your heart again with His love and grace, and understand that as far away as some prodigals have ventured, and as deep into the mire of sin as some have been, "there is always a way back." Don't judge them by your standards but understand that to refuse to enter the party is to nurture a heart that is cold and unforgiving and has become a stronghold of bitterness for the enemy to reside. It leads to serving in the field with no inner joy or freedom of spirit. Listen to the music of heaven again; angels rejoice in the parties in eternity when one sinner repents. Don't miss out on the celebrations. Next time a prodigal returns either to your home or your church family, welcome them back and give them all the encouragement and love you can; they will need it, and in doing so, you will be blessed.

I want to conclude with a remarkable true story and experience that my wife Val had just a few years ago. When her elderly mother became sick and needed to be looked after, my wife would spend several months through the year with her. This would mean flying over to England and being her full-time caregiver. When she returned to the United States for a while, her brother Barry would take over, and so between them, they did a great job of caring for their mother, who all her life had served the Lord and had for many years lived on her own after her husband had died. It was just prior to one of these trips that she felt the Lord speak to her with a message that was quite unusual although she never mentioned this to me at the time. Val and I had gone through probably what we could only say was the worst trial we had ever encountered. I am not at liberty to divulge what this was in this book although our close friends will remember the onslaught from what seemed to be from the pit of hell upon our family. We got to a point where we had prayed so much and for so long that we were exhausted and wondered in what way we could pray most effectively. My wife flew off to England again to look after her mother, and it was while she was out shopping for her mother that she felt the Lord speak the same message to her. Like many of us, if the message seems strange and out of the ordinary, most of us ask ourselves the question, "Is this God, or is it me?"

I really need to stress the point here that we do believe God can speak in various ways, but neither of us are the kind of people that profess to hear God speaking every day, especially with words like I am about to share. We both have had specific guidance in major decisions we have made together in life, and we both have known many times when we felt the Lord is prompting us to do certain things. But this word that Val received was quite out of the ordinary and was one of those times when one needs to be sure that this was the voice of God. A third time this message came with exactly the same words, this time she was upstairs at her mother's home, and the message was as follows: "Go to Wigan Park and sit beside the pond, and there I will speak to you."

Val's mother lived in the North West England in a town called Leigh about twenty miles from Manchester and a similar distance from Liverpool. Wigan was the town where Val was born and brought up and was just eight miles away. She knew the park very well, as when we were first married, we lived just around the corner from what is called Mesnes Park. It's a large park just off the center of the town, and one of its features is that it has a pond. Parents would often take their children to this pond to feed the ducks in the summer time. Around this pond were a number of benches so people could sit and relax during the warmer weather.

However, when Val was over with her mother, it was October, and it was a rather damp and dreary kind of day. I remember her calling me and asking me what I thought she should do. She related the message she believed the Lord had spoken to her and that she had to go to Wigan Park. I immediately told her to go and be obedient to the message, although I guess we both wondered as to why God would ask her go to the park to speak to her. That part was pretty difficult to understand, but at the same time feeling convinced this was the Lord speaking, there was a certain amount of excitement, as well as being a little apprehensive.

She had to take a bus ride to get to the park in Wigan, and as she walked toward the park from the town center, she had in her handbag a small New Testament and a little book by David Wilkerson she had been reading. She thought she would make her way to one of the park benches by the pond and decided she would sit and read, and maybe this is how God would speak to her. It was the middle of the morning on a damp October day and the park was deserted apart from in the distance a few workmen who were busy tidying up some of the flower beds. Val sat down in the middle of one of those benches, reached into her bag, and pulled out her New Testament. She had only been reading for a few minutes when two young men, probably about eighteen years of age, came walking into the park making their way toward the pond. Their loud talk and rather boisterous ways shattered the quietness of the park, and there was no mistaking they were around, as they pushed and shoved each laughing loudly. Please keep in mind there was a number of benches situated around this pond, but as they walked by the bench where Val was sat, one of them turned back and said, "I'm sitting here," and promptly sat down beside Val. This made her a little nervous especially when the other young man came and sat the other side of her. She held onto her bag very tightly and thought to herself, rather than sit there afraid, *I may as well engage them in conversation.* She asked them where they lived to which one replied, "Leigh," which was the same town Val's mother lived in. The conversation carried on for a while especially when they asked her where she was from and she told them she lived near Chicago!

One of the young men eventually pulled up his jean just above his ankle and said, "Look what I've got to wear." He revealed he had an ankle bracelet so that he could be tracked by the police. "I have to appear in court soon, but it's not fair. I didn't do anything to break the law. It was some of my friends," he said and pleaded his innocence.

Val listened for a while and then replied, "I have a friend who was accused of many things, and he was innocent too. He eventually died after they had mistreated him. Do you want me to tell you his name?" she asked.

They both quickly replied, "Yes, what was his name?"

Val looked directly into their faces and said, "Jesus."

One of the young men quickly asked, "Do you mean God?"

"Yes, that's right," Val replied. She then told them all about the crucifixion of Christ and why this had to happen. She then posed a question to them, "Do you ever wonder why you are on this earth and what the purpose of your life is?"

The young man with the ankle bracelet immediately jumped up and said, "I don't believe you are asking that question. That is exactly what I was asking myself this morning."

It was very similar to the question the angel asked Hagar, "Where did you come from and where are you going?" She challenged them with the issues of heaven and hell and the choice that has to be made.

The young men listened intently, and then one of them asked if she believed in the devil, "Of course," Val replied. "He is very real personality too." The young men then began telling her that in one of their friends apartment a short time ago, they had brought out an Ouija board, and strange things started to happen which really frightened him. He told her as they were busy with the Ouija board, a glass suddenly flew across the room and smashed into a wall. This experience had obviously impacted this young man so much so that he decided he would research on the Internet the reality of demons. He began to share what he had researched and asked if Val believed that certain demons could be dispatched to particular situations? She told him she did. It was then he said something regarding demonic strategies and how demons can manipulate situations that Val felt this is what the Lord wanted her to hear and was actually a confirmation to how we had felt we should pray. She told them both in no uncertain terms that they were playing around with a very evil personality called the devil who wanted to destroy their lives and that they should have no further part in any Ouija board activities. She also made it abundantly clear to them that God loved them and had a plan and purpose for their lives. They both listened intently as they heard the message of salvation and what they needed to do by way of repentance of their sin and to turn in faith to the Lord Jesus Christ. She asked them if they knew of the church where she used to attend years ago, they said they did. She wrote the name and address of the church and the pastor's name on a little piece of paper and handed it to them and encouraged them to attend. One of the boys wrapped the little piece of paper up, and so that he wouldn't lose it, he placed it in the back of his phone. Val assured them she would be praying for them as the young men walked away.

When Val heard the Lord speak on those three separate occasions, "Go to Wigan Park, and I will speak to you there," she had no idea how this would happen, but as we looked back, we were once again amazed at the goodness and grace of God and how this had all taken place.

God brought two young men who had probably never heard the gospel before in their lives into a park on a damp October day, to sit on a seat beside my wife, although all the other benches were all empty. He used these young men to confirm certain things to her regarding satanic strategies and as to how to pray more effectively, at the same time gave the young men the opportunity of hearing the gospel. God who knows all things, and who answers prayer, can arrange situations and meetings that all fall into the great plan and purpose of God.

I would love to finish that story by telling you that the two young men went to that church and gave their lives over to Jesus Christ, but I don't know if that happened; perhaps they did, or maybe at some future time in their lives they will. One thing is certain, those two young prodigals had a choice to make after that meeting in the park.

All prodigals have to make choices; we all do every day of our lives, but some choices are more important than others.

Thank you for taking time to read this book. My prayer is that it has been helpful to you and a blessing, perhaps challenging in various ways, but making the right choices is all important. The prodigal son made a choice; it was either to stay in the pigsty or make the journey home; thankfully, he made the right choice. The elder brother who we called the second prodigal also had a choice; sadly, he chose not to celebrate his brother's homecoming, and he missed the party and lived a life void of grace. Wasted years can be a thing of the past as God's abundant restoration takes place. Make the right choice, because "destiny is a matter of choice not chance."

I close with the words of a song written by Lauren Daigle, "Dry Bones":

> God of endless mercy,
> God of unrelenting love,
> Rescue every daughter,
> Bring us back our wayward sons.

My prayer is "may every prodigal son and daughter be restored, and may the breath of God reach into every dark valley where there seems to be no hope, bringing life and resurrection. May families that have known the pain of disconnect know the joy of restoration and celebration."

If you are praying for a prodigal, prepare also in faith, and if you are the returning prodigal, don't let anything deter you on the way. The party and celebration awaits because "there is always a way back."

Please see notes for discussion for small groups below.

Discussions for
Small Groups

This book can also be used as a tool for discussion in home groups or small groups. Small groups have been used all over the world in many different cultures. They can be a great evangelistic tool and also as a method for discipleship. Truths can be underlined; misunderstandings can be corrected, and people can learn from the forum of being able to ask questions and discuss together some of the important topics the book brings out. I hope you will find these topics and discussions helpful.

Chapter 1: Walking Away Is Never Immediate

Read together Luke 15.

1. Would you agree or disagree with the assumption that "walking away is never immediate" or as stated in the first chapter "almost never immediate"? In the story of the prodigal son, he walked away from his father, but there are many other scenarios we could mention, i.e., walking away from church, etc.
2. In today's culture, why do you think prodigals leave the Father's presence, and where does the desire to leave begin?
3. What are the practical ways that can be implemented to avoid the falling away from the faith of?
4. If there have been times in your own experience where you may feel that your walk with the Lord was not as intimate and close as it was, what steps did you take to rectify this?
5. With the characters that are mentioned in chapter 1, where do you think the problem began that led to their prodigal behavior?

Demas (2 Timothy 4:10)
Jacob (Genesis 25:28 and 27:1–10)
King David (2 Samuel v1–5)

Chapter 2: Inheritance without the Father's Presence

Read Luke 15:13.

1. In Luke11, Jesus taught His disciples to pray and to call God their Father. See also Romans 8:15, "For you did not receive the spirit of bondage again to fear but you received the Spirit of adoption by whom we cry out Abba Father. Discuss the phrase "spirit of adoption" and your own experience of understanding and relating to God as your Father. Was it difficult for you to relate to God as your Father? Share any practical ways the experience of this truth has made in your life.

2. What value did the Apostle Paul place on the Father's presence and knowing Him? Read Philippians 3:7–14. What do you think Paul meant when he referred to "counting all things loss for the excellency of the knowledge of Christ (verse 8)?

3. Relate anything in your own life that you have counted loss in order that you may know Christ better.

4. How and why do you think Paul's prayer in Ephesians 1:17–22 is important to pray for all believers?

5. From the phrase used in chapter 2 "God is seeking a bride not a girlfriend," what practical things can we draw from this?

6. In this chapter, there are two true stories of people "encountering God"—New Zealand pastors and Brazil "encounter weekend." Do you feel "the encountering of God" is a missing element in modern Christianity, and can you relate any such experiences?

Chapter 3: A Life That Is Empty Is Open for Deception

1. Read Revelation 12:9, ". . . the devil deceives the world." Discuss some of the main deceptions that people are subjected to in our culture.
2. Read Isaiah 42:3, Matthew 12:20, and Luke 4:18–19. Discuss the meaning of these verses and the ministry and purpose of God that these verses reveal.
3. Discuss the quote by Johann Hari re. Portugal's drug problems and the connection with loneliness. Quote: "We humans have created societies where it is easier for people to be cut off from all human connections than ever before."
4. What can individual believers and the church do to provide connections and counteract loneliness?
5. Discuss how so-called political correctness has sought to stifle the message of the gospel.
6. Read Matthew 6:25–34.

    The prodigal son was eager to receive his inheritance (money).

    Discuss Jesus's teaching relative to money in this passage.

Chapter 4: Prodigal Living in a Prodigal World

"And not many days after the younger son gathered altogether, journeyed to a far country, and there wasted his possessions with prodigal living" (Luke 15:13).

The definition of the word *prodigal* is to be wastefully or recklessly extravagant. The prodigal had set his mind on prodigal living.

Read also Genesis 13:10, "Lot lifted up his eyes and saw all the plain of Jordan that it was well watered everywhere before the Lord destroyed Sodom and Gomorrah, like the garden of the Lord."

"Lot pitched his tent even as far as Sodom." (Genesis 13:13).

1. Discuss the close connection in living near to the borders of sin/immorality and moving into the midst. What can we learn from the story of Lot?

2. Paul gives a description of a prodigal world in Ephesians 2:1–3. Discuss the principle of how the devil works through the lusts of the flesh and the desires of the mind, and how do you think this has become more intense in this generation?

3. Peter writes of the transformation that takes place in the life of the believer and the difficulty the world has in understanding this (1Peter 4:3). Relate your own experience of this and the response of unbelievers to your new lifestyle.

4. In the quote from Stephen Harris' book, *Truth Decay,* he refers to the landmark of the Ten Commandments that have been removed from some public places. What are the landmarks or principles that we should make sure are not removed from "family life" and also from "church life."

5. Note the phrase that the prodigal used when asking for his inheritance, ". . . give me." (Luke 15:12). Self-centeredness is the root that breeds deception and turns the heart away from the Father. As believers, what can we do to keep our hearts free from this?

Chapter 5: A Wasted Inheritance

Read John 10:10, John 3:16, Romans 6:23

"For if when we were enemies we were reconciled to God through the death of His Son, much more having been reconciled we shall be saved by His life" (Romans 5:10).

1. What do you think Paul meant by the phrase "we shall be saved by His life"? This is obviously not referring to the initial moment of salvation.
2. What do you think Jesus meant in John 10v10 re. abundant life? Would you say that you experience this and if so in what way?
3. From the quote of Alaina Tweddale for Prudential in the article entitled "Why 7 in 10 People Suddenly Inherit Money and Lose It All," she writes that an inheritance that we have not worked for is typically spent more loosely. In Romans 8:17, the Message calls the believer's inheritance "an unbelievable inheritance." What is your understanding of this verse?
4. In the story of Esther referred to in this book, Esther goes uninvited to meet with the King. The golden scepter was held out to her so that she could approach him (Esther 5:2). Relate any experiences when in your time of need you have found help from the Lord who invites us into His presence (Hebrews 4:16).
5. Why do you think that there are some believers who never seem to enjoy their spiritual inheritance and as a result live below the level of faith and expectancy?

Chapter 6: When God Sends a Famine

"But when he had spent all there arose a severe famine in that land, and he began to be in want" Luke 15:14.

1. Do you agree with the thought that God in His divine providence can actually send a famine in order to bring about His purposes? Consider also Genesis 43:1, Psalm 105:16, 1 Kings 17 re. Elijah and Ahab, and 2 Chronicles 7:14.
2. Do you think that the extreme action of sending a famine is in keeping with God's character?
3. The prodigal came to a desperate point of need. Can you relate to any situations in your life or in the lives of others where need has brought them to an awareness of their spiritual need?
4. Read Isaiah 53; please note verses 5 and 10. With the words "smitten by God" and "it pleased the Lord to bruise Him," how and why could Christ be smitten and bruised and God be pleased to do this?

Chapter 7: Eating with Pigs

"He would have gladly filled his stomach with the pods that the swine ate" (Luke 15:15–16).

1. The prodigal hit rock bottom and couldn't get any lower. Many have had similar experiences but do not turn to the Father. What is the difference between those who do and those who don't?

2. According to Leviticus 11:1–23 and Deuteronomy 14:3–21, pigs were listed as an unclean animal that the Jews should never eat. The prodigal's heart was unclean! How important do you think it is for people first to see the condition of their own heart when turning to the Lord? Do you think that the message of simply asking Christ to forgive them without any revelation of the sinfulness of their heart leads to simply a mental decision rather than real salvation? Relate your own experience and why you turned to the Lord.

3. The prodigal knew at his father's house there was food and shelter. Read Psalms 78:19 and 23:5 and Song of Solomon 2:4. Do you believe God's will is to provide and bless us, and if so, what do we need to do practically, and what spiritual principles do we need to put into practice?

4. If you are going through some difficult circumstances, do you feel this has brought you closer to God, and do you feel that you can share your experience and allow the group to pray for you?

Chapter 8: Left Alone

"And no one gave him anything" (Luke 15:16).

1. Listed are the quotes on loneliness from chapter eight.

    - "When I'm alone, I think and think and think."
    - "I use sarcasm and jokes to cover up the fact that I am lonely and have bad anxiety about almost everything."
    - "Lonely is not being alone it's the feeling that no one cares."
    - "You never realize how lonely you are until it's the end of the day and you have a bunch of things to talk about and no-one to talk to."
    - "I feel I'm not anyone's first choice, neither their favorite. Even if people tell me I'm important to them, or I mean a lot to them I know there's always someone they prefer to be with. Someone they choose to be with over me and that it hurts a lot."

    Relate any experiences you may have had with loneliness and how you overcame or seek to overcome this.

2. Small groups help to foster relationships and community. In Genesis 1:26, "God said, 'Let us make man in our image . . .'" There is a quote in this chapter that states, "God created man with a community gene." Do you agree with this and why? How important is fellowship to you? We can relate to many people, but how important is it to have close friends and how has this helped you? What can the church do to better promote relationships and community?

3. The selfish old nature always wants to blame someone or something else for its sins and failings. Adam and Eve sought to push the blame away from themselves (Genesis 3:11–12). The prodigal could have tried to blame others for the mess he was in, but he didn't. Why do you think this was vitally important?

Chapter 9: The Turning Point

"But when he came to himself . . ." (Luke 15:17).

1. Read Proverbs 23:6–7. Do you struggle with renewing your mind from negative thoughts? Read Romans 12:1–3. What practical steps have you taken to overcome a negative mindset?
2. Read 1Samuel 27:1, "And David said in his heart, 'Now I shall perish someday by the hand of Saul." Discuss how this thought led to one of David's gravest mistakes that of joining the ranks of the enemy.
3. A mold is a hollow form or matrix giving a particular shape to something in a molten or plastic state. When clay is poured into a mold, once it is set, the mold can be removed, and the replica of the mold is now duplicated into clay. Discuss how the devil has engineered a mold for the human mind in order to fill it with the garbage and trash of unbelief, immorality, etc.
4. In Acts 2, the outpouring of the Holy Spirit brings dreams and visions. Discuss how a dream or vision from the Lord can have a transforming effect upon the believer's mind. Read Acts 26:19 re. Paul's vision. Read Genesis 15 re. Abraham's vision.

Chapter 10: The Path of Humility

"And I am no longer worthy to be called your son. Make me like one of your hired servants" (Luke 15:19).

1. "God resists the proud and gives grace to the humble" (James 4:6–7). Why do you think humility is necessary to resisting the devil?
2. The prodigal would have been tempted to give up on the journey home. Have you been tempted to give up in some ministry the Lord has called you to, and if so, how did you overcome this and continue to move forward?
3. Read again the scriptures and discuss this exhortation Paul uses to encourage the believers to do nothing through selfish ambition or conceit (Philippians 2:5–11).
4. Discuss these scriptures and the practical ways we can serve each other.

   - "The Son can do nothing of Himself" (John 5:19).
   - "I seek not my own glory . . ." (John 8:50).
   - "Learn of Me, for I am lowly of heart" (Matthew 11:29).
   - "Whosoever will be chief among you, let him be your servant, even as the Son of Man came to serve" (Matthew 20:27).

Chapter 11: What Had the Father Been Doing?

"But when he was a great way off his father saw him . . ." (Luke 15:20).

1. Imagine in this story, the prodigal's father had been praying for him while he was away from home. His father had probably one prayer that was his main prayer and that was for his son to return home. In Luke 1:11–19, Zechariah and Elizabeth had one prayer on their heart, and that was to have a son (John the Baptist). The angel said, "Your prayer has been heard." It was pretty obvious that Zechariah knew what prayer the angel was referring to. Can you share what your main prayer is that you constantly pray?

2. Read Exodus 17:8–16. In order to see victory and breakthrough in situations, how important do you feel it is to support one another in prayer, and how best can we do this?

3. What can we learn from Daniel 10 regarding prayer that can be hindered, and how important do you feel it is at times to abstain from certain foods or to fast?

4. Read Hebrews 11:1, "Now faith is the substance of things hoped for the evidence of things not seen . . ." The prodigal's father obviously had faith and was expecting one day his son would return. What has been the key to staying in faith and to keep praying even when the prodigals seem so far away, or the situation you are praying about doesn't seem to change? Relate your experience.

Spend some time as a group praying together for prodigals.

Chapter 12: When the Father Runs

"But when he was a great way off, his father saw him and had compassion and ran and fell on his neck and kissed him" (Luke 15:20).

1. Read Psalm 51 and note verse 3 "my sin is always before me." Also, read 2 Samuel 11:4 and 2 Samuel 12:13. Although David had sinned, his immediate response was to repent when confronted by the prophet Nathan. Why do you think David responded so quickly? How could David have avoided giving in to the temptation with Bathsheba?
2. When Jesus told the story of the prodigal son, why do you feel He placed emphasis on the prodigal's repentance first toward heaven and then his father?
3. In this chapter, we read of the father running, and a number of stories of people who became God's runners are included. Relate your own experience of who God used to be the runner who brought you to the Lord.
4. In 2 Corinthians 6:1, Paul writes that we are co-workers or co-runners with God. See also 1 Corinthians 9:24–27 "running to win"; what do you think are the practical things that we need to do for this to take place?
5. In the story of Derek Redmond and the four-hundred-meter race in the 1992 Olympics, his dad came to his aid to help him to the finish line. When believers fall back or get injured, what can we do to get them moving again to the finish line?

Chapter 13: He Didn't Get What He Was Expecting

"His father saw him and had compassion and ran and fell on his neck and kissed him" (Luke 15:20).

1. Why do you think it is hard for some people to understand how the grace of God works? Do you think it is because of our culture that rewards good behavior and punishes bad behavior that some people do not understand the grace of God? Or is it because the devil has blinded the minds of those who do not believe, or both of the above?

2. How did you discover the grace of God? Relate your own experience.

3. Grace is free but it is not cheap! Read 1 Peter 1:18–19. Please note also Isaiah 53:5–6. Do you understand the reason for Christ's suffering that it was necessary in order for the grace of God to be offered to the repentant sinner? Discuss this relative to the unchanging character of God. (Holiness demands judgment, but grace and love long to bless).

4. Read Ephesians 1:5–6. Discuss what you believe being "accepted in the beloved" means.

5. Read Matthew 18:23–35. As a recipient of the grace of God, do you struggle or have you struggled in the past with issues of forgiveness? Please ask for prayer at this point if you feel you need help in this area. When forgiving or praying a prayer of forgiveness, what importance if any should we put on how we feel afterward?

Chapter 14: It's Party Time

"Let us eat and be merry . . ." (Luke 15:22–24).

1. In Luke 15, there are two other stories, one of a lost coin and the other of a lost sheep. Think about the Pharisees who were listening and were very self-righteous. Do you think it is strange that a shepherd would leave ninety-nine sheep to search for and rescue one? What point was Jesus making?

   Quote from chapter 14:
   "Let's just consider these stories or parables for a moment. As I wrote in the introduction to this book, the context in which Jesus told these stories was that the religious leaders the Pharisees had accused Him not so much of teaching and talking to sinners but eating with them. The Jewish culture was that of a shame and honor system. The motivation behind much of what took place was to seek honor for oneself and avoid shame. The fact that the good shepherd would leave the ninety-nine sheep behind to seek the one which was lost was to portray the love, compassion, and forgiveness of God. But what about the ninety-nine sheep he left on the mountain side? Was there some sarcasm in the reference to the ninety-nine righteous persons who needed no repentance?"

2. The prodigal's father lavished him with gifts, the robe typical of the robe of righteousness (2 Corinthians 5:21). The ring is representative of belonging to the family and acceptance (1John 3:1–3). The sandals are representative of a new walk (Jeremiah 29:11). The fatted calf—food, representative of celebration time. Discuss these scriptures.

3. Discuss the party for a prostitute story in this chapter. Do you think this is the kind of church Jesus would be pleased with?

4. How can we practically help repentant sinners to feel accepted?

   What practical way can we connect with those who are not saved in order to influence them toward the kingdom?

Chapter 15: What He Thought He Would Become He Didn't

"I am no longer worthy to be called your son, make me as one of your hired servants" (Luke 15:19).

1. When you first came to know the Lord, did you have any ideas other than forgiveness and the promise of eternal life of the privileges and blessings that would be yours?
2. The prodigal could only hope to be received back as a servant, but he was welcomed as a son. Discuss the definition found in this chapter of both servants and sons and how both of these truths should be blended together in our personal lives.
3. Paul and Peter both address themselves as "bond servants" of Jesus Christ. A "bond servant" is someone who is devoted to another to the disregard of one's interests. Please note Philippians 1:1 and 2 Peter 1:1. Do you think this is a missing element in modern Christianity?
4. Would you say that the definition of a "bond servant" is the description of a true disciple?
5. Is being a "bond servant" something you have or do struggle with? If so, what are the practical ways to overcome this and to be able to present your bodies as a living sacrifice? Please note Romans 1:1.
6. Discuss Christ's servanthood (Philippians 2:5–8). Paul urges us to let this same mind to be in us. How do we practically do this?

Chapter 16: Adjustments to Restoration

"Now his older son was in the field, and as he came out of the field he heard music and dancing" (Luke 15:25).

1. The prodigal would have to come to terms with adjustments to his restoration. Often, it is the adjustments in our minds and thinking that is difficult. How can we come to terms with forgiving ourselves?
2. What scriptures are applicable to this?
3. Read 2 Corinthians 10:4–6. What do you think is meant by strongholds, and what are the spiritual weapons we must employ to tear them down?
4. Read Romans 12:1–3. Discuss the practicalities of renewing the mind and how this brings transformation. If you have experienced this, share this with the group.
5. Read Philippians 3:13. If our history is not our destiny and past failures should not be allowed to rob us of future blessing, how do we like the Apostle Paul come to the place where we forget those things which are behind and reach forth to those things which are ahead?
6. How can we as believers help returning prodigals to make the adjustments and to feel welcomed home?

Chapter 17: The Other Prodigal

"But he was angry and would not go in. Therefore his father came out to him and pleaded with him" (Luke 15:28).

1. Discuss the elder brother's attitude and why he would not go into the party, and what was the spiritual principle he was missing?
2. Read Luke 18:10–14. When we compare ourselves with others in order to gain acceptance with God, we are adopting a merit system and remove grace. This was different from pharisaical teaching; it was revolutionary! What are the qualities that the elder brother should have shown to the prodigal?
3. The elder brother's pharisaical attitude still exists and is responsible for many leaving churches or being stumbled before they arrive home! In this chapter is the story of a church in the UK where one family wanted their pastor to ask a family who had recently started attending the church to move seats because that is where they always sat. What would have been your response if you had been the pastor, and what should this family's attitude have been rather than asking if they could move seats?
4. Read Luke 10:38–42. The elder brother was serving but knew nothing of the privileges of sonship.

Mary sat at the feet of Jesus, and Martha served in the kitchen. C.H. Spurgeon said, "Go with Martha but first sit with Mary." Do you think this principle is important and why? Is it only regarded as "spiritual" to be sitting at the feet of Jesus (praying, reading, worshipping), or are the practical things that Martha was doing also "spiritual"? Can these two be blended together? And if so, relate any scriptures that would prove this point.

Chapter 18: Restoration of Wasted Years

"I will restore to you the years the locusts has eaten, the canker-worm and the caterpillar and the palmerworm my great army which I sent among you" (Joel 2:25).

1. Read 2 Timothy 4:7–8. Paul could look back and testify that since his conversion, he had never been disobedient to the heavenly vision. Since that time, he seems to have "no wasted years." Do you look back on any times through your life that you feel may fall into the category of "wasted years"? If so, what would you say would be the reason?

2. Read Joel 2:15–18. Discuss these scriptures and how we can apply them to our individual lives.

3. Read Genesis 16:16 and 17:1. Please note that there is a period of thirteen years of what seems to be silence from God. Abraham had listened to the voice of human reasoning regarding the promise of a child. Discuss how Abraham must have felt during this time period.

4. How do you feel when you seem to be in a waiting period and the promise God has made to you doesn't seem to materialize?

5. Read Joel 2:19 and 23–24. Discuss the abundance of restoration blessing and how this can apply to us. Discuss any practical things that you feel you should begin to implement in your life in order to invoke the blessings of restoration. If prayer is needed, take time to minister to one another.

Chapter 19: Where Have You Come from and Where Are You Going?

"And He said, 'Hagar Sarai's maid, where have you come from and where are you going?'" (Genesis 16:8).

1. Read Genesis 19:1–8. Discuss the change that Jesus has made in your life and the kind of life you left behind and your spiritual aspirations for the future.
2. In praying for prodigals, what are the main obstacles in prayer that you feel you have to overcome?
3. God's will is His desire, and it does not mean that automatically His desires will come to pass. Discuss this thought in the light of 2 Peter3:9).
4. God's character will never change, but He can change His mind. Discuss this thought in the light of Exodus 32:14.
5. In this chapter, I have included the story of my wife Val having a word from God that led to two young men hearing the gospel and also an answer as to how to pray in a certain situation. Can you relate to any similar experiences?
6. Close the discussion time by praying together and believing for prodigals to return.

I hope the book and the discussion pages have been a help and blessing to you. Always remember, "there is always a way back."

Bibliography

Huffpost internet edition.
The power of humanity in partnership with Dignity Health.
Article updated 01/20/2015 updated Apr. 18th 2017
'The Likely Cause of Addiction Has been Discovered and its not What You Think.
By Johann Hari author of 'Chasing The Scream' Bloomsbury ISBN 978-1-620-408902
ISBN-13: 978-16204-08919 reprint 3-1-2016

'Truth Decay' by Stephen Hales.
Riverstone Group 2016 ASIN: B0010EC03Q

Internet article by Alaina Tweddale for Prudential 4/20/17
'Why 7 in 10 People Who Suddenly Inherit Money Lose It All'.

Internet article 'Pressreader'
'Women In The Window' human trafficking.
Mail on Sunday UK Feb.11th 2018

'Building a Church of Small Groups' by Bill Donahue and Russ Robinson.
Zondervan Grand Rapids 1 Oct, 2005
ISBN 10: 03102267102
ISBN 13: 9780310267102

US News Civic/National internet article.
A First Person Account. John McCain, Prisoner of War Vietnam.
Jan.28, 2008 (11.00am).

BIBLIOGRAPHY

'Fresh Wind Fresh Fire' by Jim Cymbala and Dean Merrill.
Zondervan 2018 ISBN; 1310350603 ISBN-13: 9780310350606

Awesome Stories (internet 800 277 1381) original release Jan.31 2016. Updated Jan.19 2017.
Derek Redmond's story 'The Day That Changed My Life. Sermon Illustrations Internet.'

'A Party For a Prostitute' "The Kingdom of God is a Party' by Tony Campolo
Thomas Nelson 1990 ISBN 0849933994 ISBN -13 978084993398

'Prayer is Invading the Impossible' by Jack Hayford. (page 54).
Bridge publishing –South Plainfield New Jersey. 1977
ISBN-0-88270-2184

Cats in the Cradle song by Harry Chapin 1974 from the albumn 'Verities and Balderdash'.

About the Author

K eith and his wife, Val, travel internationally, ministering in conferences, missions, and local churches.

Keith came to faith in Christ at the age of seventeen. Initially called to the ministry as an evangelist, Keith traveled to many towns and cities around the UK, conducting evangelistic and church-planting missions. Keith and his wife, Val, have also planted and pastored several churches in the UK and are currently engaged in pastoral ministry in the United States.

They have a UK charitable trust called Ocean Wings, which helps to finance their trips to third-world countries. They minister regularly in Africa and have input into numbers of the village churches in Uganda.

Keith has also recorded two song albums, one entitled *People Need the Lord*, and the latest one, *My Dream Come True*. He is also the author of a book entitled *The Gospel We Preach* which was published in 2017

Keith and Val have two sons Mark and Paul and love spending time with them along with their wives and grandchildren.

Keith can be contacted by Messenger on Face Book and also for information and to learn more about the author and missions/conferences the Ocean Wings website is www.ocean-Wings.net.

CPSIA information can be obtained
at www.ICGtesting.com
Printed in the USA
FFHW021934041218
49711118-54146FF